SHE CAN GO
WHERE PRETTY GIRLS GO

CONSTANCE GIBSON

SHE CAN GO
WHERE PRETTY GIRLS GO

Beyond Ink
New York

SHE CAN GO
WHERE PRETTY GIRLS GO

Copyright © 2001 by Constance Gibson

All rights reserved. No part of this book may be used or reproduced in any manner whatsoever without the written permission of the publisher. Printed in the United States of America.

For information, address:
Beyond Ink
P.O. Box 1644
New York, NY 10026-1644

ISBN 0-9768166-0-1

Library of Congress Control Number: 2005903508

Published in July, 2005

Creative Consultant Deborah Gibson

Cover by Alvaro

ACKNOWLEDGEMENTS

First and always, thanks and praise to God. A special thanks to: Catherine Revland for her insight, input, and love for the arts, my niece Loreal for her support, my husband Bas for his belief in me, and my partner, consultant, and sister Deb who has been there for me from the very beginning.

Dedicated to my great-grandparents Abbey and George Cofield—for their inspiration and legacy.

CONTENTS

CARLISLE, SOUTH CAROLINA

UP THE ROAD

B.Y.O.B.

UPBEAT!

BLACK BUTTERFLY

MY JOURNEY TO ME

A NEW LIFE

GROUND CREW

STYLE ARCHITECT

LIFE'S HALL OF FAME

CARLISLE, SOUTH CAROLINA

My past had come back to claim me with a vengeance. Alone, collapsed on the floor in tears, I tried to make some sense of things. It was the New Year, the New *Century*, 2000. Slowly recuperating from burnout, I had fled a successful career in the city, my marriage, and my friends to live in the small Southern town I was born in, nearly half a century ago. My homecoming wasn't exactly welcoming. Instead of the clarity, understanding, and acceptance I was seeking, I found confusion, hurt, and rejection. It was time to accept myself even if no one else would. I pulled myself together, gained control of my thoughts. In search of questions as well as answers, I found a pen and tablet and just started writing, all day and well into the night. About things I hadn't shared with anyone: the past, all the things I had practically forgotten, the "secret." Dawn found me deep in thought, scribbling. Soon, writing every day, most of the day, things seemed to get clearer, less frightening. "What had brought me to this point?" I wondered, "full circle, back to the beginning?" It seemed so unbelievably long ago.

Nineteen-fifties Carlisle, South Carolina was a scenic rural community; carved out and nestled in the middle of Sumter National

She Can Go Where Pretty Girls Go

Forest. With a population of less than a thousand, the town had its own post office, a small hotel, three diners, a general store, a busy train depot, and recalling a not-so-distant past, a genuine old plantation, complete with antebellum mansion. Predominantly poor, uneducated, and "colored," many families took pride in prime farming and grazing lands, passed down from previous generations. Others sharecropped or braved the harsh cotton fields and orchards for wages less than twenty-five dollars a week. Though most commerce was white owned and operated, a few blacks had businesses: a store, a small diner, and for letting loose on weekends, an all-night juke joint that offered bootleg whiskey, dancing, and live gut-bucket blues.

Even though Carlisle's residents coexisted somewhat peacefully, segregation was enforced. Like most public places, the train depot had a "white" section and a "colored" section. Seating on board the train was separate as well. Schools were segregated. Ever since theirs was shut down in the forties, blacks were bused to nearby Santuc while an all-white school stood right in the middle of town. Frustrated, many young blacks headed North, especially to the Midwest, in search of a chance. Others could only hope and dream.

At Union County Courthouse in 1952, my nineteen-year-old mother Effie Lee Crosby married Arlee "Red Gip" Gibson, twenty-two. Pretty, Effie was a little over five feet tall and fair-skinned, with curly black hair, dark eyes, and a slight stutter. She already had two children: her newborn son Lester, by Arlee, and a four-year-old daughter named Ernestine, by a former beau when she was just fifteen. Ernestine lived with Effie's mother in the family house just beyond the railroad tracks. "I—I was so stupid back in them days," Effie recalled, slowly shaking her head. "Mama never tol' us kids nothin' 'bout sex. Just tol' us not to be messin' 'round. I didn't even know how I was gittin' pregnant 'til I had my third child!" Nicknamed "Red Gip" because of his light, sparsely freckled complexion, Effie's slim handsome husband stood over six feet tall. Neither had completed school. "Ba—back then kids left school early to work and to help out the fam'ly," recalled my mother. She made it to the tenth grade; her husband dropped out in grammar school. "Red Gip couldn't read and could only write his name, but he could sho' count money real good," she laughed.

The marriage got off to a rough start. The couple moved in with Red Gip's parents in the Brooklyn section of Carlisle. That's where I was born on a stormy May night in 1953 with the help of a cousin and town midwife, Hattie Tucker. Because of a striking resemblance, I was named after my father. Like many men in town, Arlee "Red Gip" Gibson drank—heavily. Effie recalled seeing little of him "and even less of his paychecks!" from a job hauling puck wood. "He was givin' money to his wine-head girlfriends! His Mama helped me out wit' y'all!" In a marriage alone, penniless, with small stomachs to fill, she felt hopeless and trapped. Unhappy with his on-again, off-again low-paying job and burning out on drinking, Red Gip had also come to a dead end. After hearing of his troubles, a sister who had married and left town to settle in Aliquippa, Pennsylvania invited him there to look for work. He gladly accepted.

"I sen' fa ya soon as I fine somethin'," he told his young wife. "Maybe things 'ill be better there. Sho' can't be no worse then here."

It didn't take long for Red Gip to get settled. After securing employment at J & L Steel and a place to live, he sent for his family. "Thank you, Lord!" Effie shouted, excited to be leaving Carlisle.

She asked her mother to keep all her children until she got settled but was quickly and firmly told, "Been lookin' after Ernestine since she was a baby. No ifs, ands, or buts: You take the other younguns on wit' *you*."

She Can Go Where Pretty Girls Go

Reunited with her husband and in new surroundings, Effie was optimistic. Though the neighborhood was a slum, the weather gray most days, and she had no friends as yet, Aliquippa was better than back home—"A chance," she thought. She set up house in the couple's new two-bedroom tenement and cared for their two children. For once, Red Gip was being responsible: working, bringing his checks home, and staying in nights. Within four months Effie became pregnant and in the following year gave birth to her fourth child, a beautiful daughter she named Deborah. Things were going well. For the first time in the marriage Effie felt some sort of stability, like she was getting somewhere, "like things might turn out right after all." But unfortunately, they didn't. Six months after the birth of their daughter, Red Gip's demons returned along with the booze, women, stay-out-all-nights, and absentee paychecks. "It got so bad I had to depen' on neighbors to help feed my kids," said Effie, almost crying. "I had finally had enough!"

When her infant turned one Effie decided to leave Aliquippa and join three sisters settled in Cleveland, Ohio. Two of them owned businesses: a diner and ice-cream parlor. All Effie needed was someone to keep her children until she got settled. When her mother and in-laws refused to help, she decided to take my five-year-old brother Lester with her and leave my baby sister and me with our father. "But why Lester gitta go and we don't?" I cried.

"Ca—cause he five and need ta go to school. Baby, I gotta do this. I promise I'll be back for you and ya sistah soon." My father was even more upset with the arrangement than I was, but Effie's mind was made up.

The very evening Mama left for Cleveland, a friend of Daddy's drove him, Deb, and me to a tenement across town. With his friend waiting and the motor running, Daddy took us to the front door and began pounding. "Open up! It's Red Gip!" he shouted.

Carlisle, South Carolina

No one answered. "Open up, dammit!" he yelled again. There was still no answer. Determined, he turned the doorknob. When he discovered it had been left unlocked, Daddy grinned. We entered cautiously, my father leading the way. It was pitch black inside and no one seemed to be home. "Sit over in dat chair!" Daddy ordered me before placing my baby sister in my lap. "Now y'all be good 'til I git back!" he said. Then he left.

After what seemed like an eternity, someone came to the front door. "Please let it be Daddy," I whispered. Instead, a couple and two small children walked in. They were startled when they switched on the light and discovered my sister and me; frightened, still seated in the chair my father left us in. The couple turned out to be Daddy's sister Queen and her husband Hubbard. She was angry. He was furious!

"Where yo daddy?" he bellowed.

Frightened, I mumbled, "Don't know."

Turning to my aunt, he shouted, "I know he don't think he gonna jus' dump his kids here and run off! Uh Uhhh! I know he don't think *that*!" We were hurried to bed while an angry Uncle Hubbard went out to search for our father.

Space in the small two-bedroom apartment was limited; so my sister and I slept on a rollaway bed in a boiler room in the back. Doubling as the laundry room, the cramped space smelled dank, like dirty wet clothes that had mildewed. Exhausted, Deb passed out as soon as her tiny head hit the pillow. I stayed awake, hoping Daddy was coming back for us. By morning it became apparent that he never was.

My aunt and uncle resented our presence. "I got kids of my own to support," Aunt Queen would say. Consequently, my sister and I received little. We repeatedly wore the clothes we arrived in. My ankles stayed raw and blistered from scraping against the backs of shoes a size too small. I was only four but did my best

She Can Go Where Pretty Girls Go

to help care for my one-year-old sister, often changing diapers and washing her as I had seen my mother do a hundred times. The biggest challenges were combing and braiding her long thick hair. Though it had no head, I made her a doll from discarded scraps of fabric. I didn't mind the responsibility. She was all I had left. Sadly, I was resigned to the fact that my father wasn't returning, but held out hope my mother would. I often dreamt of her standing over our bed crying.

One night, while dreaming about her, I was suddenly awakened by my mother's voice, arguing with my aunt and uncle. As I opened my eyes, a hand with red nails parted the curtained doorway. "Mama?" I whispered, rubbing my eyes to make sure I wasn't still dreaming.

"It's me, baby," she said as we hugged. "Y'all okay? Now git some clothes on while I dress ya sistah." Mama broke down in tears when she saw our worn tight clothing and run-over shoes. "I—I'm so sorry. I jus' found out where y'all was, then had a problem wit' your aunt and uncle. Went to court tryin' to say I was a unfit mother! My friend Mr. Leo was nice enough to let me have a couple a dollars to come git y'all. Your Aunt Edna and me rode all night long. Hurry up! She waitin' out in the car." I dressed as fast as I could. Deb and I had been in that place for over a year.

The reunion with our brother in Cleveland, Ohio, sadly, lasted only a few short months. My mother shared the apartment with a lady who hadn't minded one child in the small two-bedroom walk-up, but three were out of the question. We had to move in with Mama's oldest sister and her husband, across the street from their diner. I'm not sure what happened but our stay was brief. Unable to afford a place of her own, Mama sent all three of us to live with our father's parents, back in Carlisle. "Jus' for a li'l while," she promised. "I'll sen' for y'all soon as I git settled." It would be my fourth move in less than two years and another separation from my mother.

I was five when we returned South to live with our paternal grandparents. The time that Lester, Deb, and I spent on their small farm was a stable, nurturing period. Surrounded by forest, the main house was an old unpainted wooden structure with a roof made of tin. No electricity—oil lamps were used for lighting and wood-burning fireplaces provided heat. No plumbing—drinking, dishwashing, and bathing water (for the portable tin tub) was "toted" in from a nearby well. Food was stored in an "ice box," blocks of ice its source of refrigeration. Except for the kitchen, which was decorated with pretty flowered wallpaper, old newspaper served as wall covering as well as insulation in all three bedrooms, each furnished with large wooden armoires and metal-framed beds covered in Grandma's colorful handmade quilts. The living room housed her prized possession, a manual sewing machine on which she made the family's clothing. Serving as nighttime toilets, "slop jars" (large buckets) were placed throughout the house at bedtime and emptied into a gully in the morning. During the day we used the outhouse, an enclosed wooden shed situated away from the house. Old newspaper was used as toilet paper.

Grandma and Granddaddy were sharecroppers, honest and hard working. A short stout dark-skinned woman with a round pleasant face and ready smile, Grandma Eula Bell's graying hair was arranged in three plaits. She always wore dresses, even when working in the fields. Without formal schooling, married at thirteen, and the mother of thirteen, she reminded us daily, "School-in' very impotent. Spesly fa colored chulluns. Don't be like Grandma and Granddaddy. Farmin' longggg hard work!" With a voice like an angel, Eula Bell Hodges-Gibson sang as she toiled; old spirituals and funny little songs she had learned from her mother: like "Mary and Mack" and "John Brown Baby Got a Cold Upon His

Chest." She rose before dawn to start breakfast, deliciously cooked on a wood burning cast iron stove. It usually consisted of fat back from our hogs, eggs from the chicken coop, hominy grits, and flour bread. On occasion we were treated to a cup of coffee, but not often because Grandma said laughingly, "Don't y'all chulluns know coffee make ya black?"

"Fa real Grandma?" I would ask.

"How ya thank I got dis way?" She laughed even louder. After breakfast Grandma got us off to school, started dinner, cleaned house, swept the dirt front yard with her handmade straw broom, and tended the gardens. Using a washboard and homemade lye soap, she then hand-washed clothes outside in an iron kettle elevated over a small pile of slow-burning cedar. The harsh and pungent lye soap was used for cleaning and bathing as well.

Like Grandma, Granddaddy also worked hard, usually from sunup to sundown. Allen "Bo-cat" Gibson—tall, lanky, and serious, with fair skin and salt-and-pepper hair—was always dressed in overalls and work boots. With a single mule he plowed the family's three large gardens and vast cornfield. He also tended the animals and did the hunting, which provided most of our meat. Armed with a big old shotgun and four "coon" dogs, he started for the woods at daybreak. "Mama?" he'd say to his wife, "if all go good, we gonna be havin' rabbit, possum, or coon for dinna. If not, squirrels, frog legs, or birds 'ill have ta do."

"We thank God fa whatever we gits," she would reply.

We children also had chores. After school my brother and I helped feed the animals: hogs, chickens, Thanksgiving turkeys, dogs, and Granddaddy's ornery old mule. We also chopped wood, milked cows, churned butter, and did our share in the gardens. My favorite job was picking blackberries, which grew wild in the woods. Used for Grandma's killer cobblers, they were served with after-church Sunday dinners.

Carlisle, South Carolina

Attending church was mandatory. We belonged to African Methodist Episcopal, a modest one-room brick building with stained glass windows and old-style belfry. From his ornate oak pulpit, our preacher half-spoke, half-sang his spirited sermon, jumping up and down and running in place, occasionally wiping his brow with the ever-present white handkerchief. Fueled by the reverend's intensity and filled with the Holy Ghost, the congregation jumped, hollered, and on occasion fainted. Grandma would shout, doing a combination skip and tap dance up and down the aisle. "Hal-le-luuu-jah! Thank ya Lawd Jeeesus!" It was one of my most vivid memories of her.

I only have a few memories of my father. Although he had moved back to Carlisle from Pennsylvania, we didn't see much of him. We visited once while he was doing time on the chain gang. For what, no one seems to remember. Shackled and dressed in black-and-white stripes, he told my brother and me, "Stay outta places like dis!" It was the only advice I remember him passing on. I don't recall him ever hugging us, or showing any kind of affection; though he sometime playfully tugged at my sister's long pigtails. My fondest memories are of Red Gip in his baseball uniform. Summertime baseball games were a big event, played at the town's park on Saturdays. Children played, menfolk drank liquor and spun tall tales, and women cooked as they served up the latest gossip. Known for his lightning-quick curve balls, my father became a local hero as pitcher for the Carlisle Sluggers. After the games, Grandma Eula Bell would usually take my brother, sister, and me to our other grandmother's house, where we stayed for the rest of the weekend.

Many weekends were spent with our maternal grandmother, Annie Bell Cofield-Crosby, who lived within walking distance just beyond the railroad tracks. The four acres and five-room house in which she lived were purchased by her and late husband, Douglas Crosby in the early forties. As well as getting a chance to see our older sister, who lived with our grandmother, many of our first cousins spent weekends there. We shot marbles, pitched horseshoes, stepped to rhymes, and spent hours watching our grandmother's floor-model black and white television set. It was one of only a few TVs in town and Mama Annie Bell treated it like a long-lost treasure. She especially loved wrestling. Her favorite wrestler was a black man named Bobo Brazil, known for head-butting opponents with his signature "coco butt." Mama Annie Bell often got carried away during the bouts. Springing from her seat, she thrashed about, yelling at the screen, "Knock yo head up 'gainst his, Bobo! Coco butt em mannn!"

Slender, with smooth tan skin, and in her early sixties, Mama Annie Bell had the stamina of a woman twenty years her junior. She bore nine children whom she supported by working in the orchards, picking peaches. The daughter of a half-white father and half-Indian mother, she once had coal black hair so long she could sit on it, but she cut it after it whitened and fell out during a bout with typhoid fever. But Mama Annie Bell still looked good for her age. She preferred pants to dresses and sashayed sexily when she walked. She also had a sassy sense of humor. Once, someone asked her, "Miss Annie Bell? At what age do a person lose they desire for sex?"

Her immediate reply was, "I don't know, baby. You gotta ax somebody older den me."

Mama Annie Bell was also said to had been "born with a veil over her face" and the "seventh daughter of a seventh daughter." Supposedly, she had the power to glimpse into the future and even see ghosts. Her predictions were mostly about someone getting pregnant or dying and usually came in the form of dreams. "Dreamt 'bout a neckit woman last night," she'd say. "Sho' sign a death!" Needless to say, no one was ever eager to hear any of her dreams—especially me.

Carlisle, South Carolina

I *dreaded* going out into the pitch-black night to fetch firewood with Mama Annie Bell. About sixty feet behind her house, just a few steps from the woodpiles, was a seventeenth-century cemetery with thirteen graves. Some were marked with large tablet-shaped tombstones, others with small rocks. I was always relieved when we returned from the woodpiles without incident. One night, as we hurried back to the house, our arms full of wood, Mama Annie Bell stopped suddenly. I stopped too, then slowly looked back at her. She just stood there frozen, gazing at the fence that separated the yard from the sugar cane field. "Wha—what is it, Mama Annie Bell?" I asked, not really wanting to know.

"Shhh! You see dat, chile?" she whispered.

"Uh uh."

"You didn't see dat big white dog jump straight thru dat fence?"

"No."

"Look! Der he go agin!" Careful *not* to look, I jetted for the front door, sticks of wood flying in all directions.

I was afraid of Mama Annie Bell's house, as were most of the kids. There was a room in back that was bolted shut. It had been that way for years. When I questioned my grandmother about the mysterious room, she simply replied, "Hants!" That was what folks in town called ghosts. Stories of mystical healings, voodoo, and ghosts were prevalent in Carlisle. The town's most talked about ghost was "Happy Dog," a giant white canine with glowing red eyes that had supposedly been haunting the area for decades and been sighted by many. Years later, explaining why the "back room" was off-limits, my mother told me of an incident that involved my father. She and he had slept there whenever they stayed overnight. One night they were in bed sound asleep when suddenly, my father woke up, jumped out of bed, and ran from the room screaming. Trembling, he told my mother and grandmother, "A grea' big ol' white dog jumped at me, den disappeared in thin air!" There had been previous incidents so Mama Annie Bell put a big iron bolt on the door, forbidding anyone to enter. The room remained undisturbed for over twenty-five years.

My mother told of another incident that occurred in the house—concerning my oldest sister. Known by the kids in town as "Micey," Ernestine was petite and pretty with long jet-black hair and a fiery temper. She also had scars over a portion of her upper body—from an accident that occurred when she was just four. Ernestine was hand-drying a handkerchief by the fireplace in our grandmother's bedroom. She got too close and it caught on fire. Trying to put it out, she shook the burning cloth, causing her dress to catch fire. The flames spread rapidly to her chest. Hearing the screams, my mother ran from the back of the house. When she discovered her child on fire, she yelled for help as she yanked a spread from the bed. She quickly wrapped her daughter in it, then rolled her on the floor until the flames went out. Ernestine was rushed to the nearest hospital, fifteen miles away, in a neighbor's car. After hours of treatment and agonized waiting the doctor gave his diagnosis. It was devastating! Ernestine had suffered third-degree burns on her upper body and wasn't expected to survive the next six months. There was little more the doctor could do. After a few weeks in the hospital Ernestine was allowed to return home. Dealing with unbearable pain as well as emitting fluids and a foul smell, she needed round-the-clock care. My mother nursed her first-born, keeping the wounds clean and constantly changing bandages. If Ernestine's suffering was heartbreaking for my mother, it was devastating for my grandmother. She refused to accept the doctor's death sentence and sent for the highly respected "Dutch woman," known for her great healing powers. Mama Annie Bell pleaded, "I don't care what it take or what it cos'. Jus' make my baby well agin!"

Accompanied by Aunt Elneder, my sister was taken to a small shack just outside of town. The healer gathered all kinds of roots

Carlisle, South Carolina

and herbs from the woods. Then, chanting in a trance like state in "Dutch," she applied them to my sister's scorched body. Fluids began to slowly ooze from her burns. Throughout the procedure, which went on for hours, the healer chanted, gently massaging with the strange concoction. When Ernestine finally returned home the family was astonished to find her burns no longer reeked or leaked fluids. With daily applications of a salve the Dutch woman left, my sister's burns healed and she regained full health. Doctors were unable to explain the miraculous recovery.

Out of many unexplained mysteries surrounding the house, the one most curious to me was—why were there no reminders of my grandfather in my grandmother's house: no pictures, no papers—*nothing*? The family rarely spoke of him. My only memory of my maternal grandfather is of him lying in a coffin, my mother crying over his body. Five-seven, muscular, and fair-skinned, Douglas Crosby had worked as a carpenter but was less than responsible toward his family. "Daddy was meannn!" my mother recalled sadly. "One time he beat my sistahs jus' for losing at cards! Another time he choked Mama so bad it was awhile before she was able to talk right!" She told one particularly chilling story about him.

My grandfather was having an affair with the next-door neighbor, who was also married. They flaunted the liaison right under their spouses' noses. When his mistress's husband finally got fed up and went to my grandfather's house to confront him, Douglas went berserk! He began yelling obscenities and ran inside the house, returning moments later with a loaded gun. At close range, he then aimed the pistol at the man's head and opened fire. Douglas was imprisoned only seven years for the brutal killing. Upon his release he moved into the house of his mistress and the man he murdered. Until his death at age sixty-five, my grandmother endured living right next door to her husband and his mistress

She Can Go Where Pretty Girls Go

amidst their constant taunts. Perhaps *that* was one of the reasons there were no reminders of my grandfather in my grandmother's house.

It was a warm spring Saturday afternoon when our mother returned to Carlisle. As my brother, sisters, and I rushed to the house in answer to Mama Annie Bell's call, we spotted her, standing on the porch, dressed up in a pretty red dress and heels. Mama Annie Bell said she looked and smelled like new money. Her two front teeth rimmed in gold, our mother smiled, "I missed y'all so much." Then she hugged and kissed us. She smelled sweet, like flowers right after the rain. It had been three years since we last saw her. We weren't sure how to react so we stayed quiet, only answering "Yes Ma'am" and "No Ma'am" to a barrage of questions.

"Y'all been good? Mind your Grandma? Doin' good in school?"

Not yet at ease, Ernestine, Lester, Deb, and I huddled, still barely speaking. In an attempt to break our silence our mother unpacked a brand-new portable record player and small stack of forty-fives. Then she put on Mary Well's, "Bye Bye Baby" and started dancing. "Dance wit' Mama, baby!" she said, grabbing my hand. "You hip to the Cleveland jive?" Hesitant at first, I bowed my head and half smiled. Secular music and dancing weren't allowed at Grandma Eula Bell's, although I did sneak and do the "twist" on the school stage once, to the delight of fellow classmates. After some coaxing, I finally danced with my mother, and to her delight did every step she showed me—and improvised with a few of my own. "Work out, baby! You can really dance!" she shouted. "Where you learn to move like that?"

"I 'on know. I kin jus' do it," I answered. Feeling more at ease, I asked, "Mama, could you please take me back wit you so I could learn the Cleveland jive?" With tears in her eyes, she laughed. Three days later, Mama took Lester, Deb, and me back with her to Cleveland, Ohio. My eldest sister Ernestine remained in Carlisle with Mama Annie Bell, who had cared for her most of her life.

It was difficult saying good-bye to Ernestine and Mama Annie Bell. It was even harder leaving Granddaddy and Grandma Eula Bell. "Y'all be good now, and be real careful up the road," cried Grandma. My grandparents had done an excellent job caring for us and I would miss them dearly, but I was excited to be leaving for the big city and, finally, to be with my mother.

UP THE ROAD

I was nine when we arrived in Cleveland during the summer of 1962. Mama had secured a small three-room flat on LaGrange Street in an inner-city neighborhood called Hough. Nicknamed "Rough Hough," conditions were filthy. There were so many rats roaming the garbage-strewn alleyways and sometimes our building, kids with slingshots used them for target practice. Muggings were also a problem. "Don't let nobody take my money!" Mama warned before sending us to the store, just four blocks away. I had already been robbed twice. Hough was indeed rough but conditions were far better than down South. At least we had electricity, indoor plumbing, and no strenuous farm chores. We also had Aunt Edna.

Mama's sister Edna Brown had been in Cleveland five years and, with her husband Joe, stayed only two blocks away, on Linwood. Light, glamorous, and stacked, with bleached hair worn up in a French roll, she favored tight dresses and pointy spiked heels. With two years of business school Aunt Edna was the most educated of my mother's four sisters. She owned an ice-cream parlor right around the corner from us, where Lester, Deb, and I helped out for a dollar each and all the ice cream we could stomach. Next door was the Astor Theatre where I spent most of my earnings. I must have seen my first movie ever, *Whatever Happened to Baby Jane,* starring Bette Davis and Joan Crawford, at least twenty times.

In addition to the ice-cream parlor, Aunt Edna ran an after-hours joint from her spacious fifties contemporary apartment. The largest room had been converted to a nightclub, complete with bar, jukebox, and dance floor. During weekend sleepovers I'd sneak and stay up late, dancing in the mirror to Sam Cooke, Ray Charles, Bobby "Blue" Bland, and Chubby Checker. Unexpectedly, one night my aunt abruptly opened my bedroom door. "Busted!" she shouted, scaring me half to death. Grinning sheepishly, I dived back into bed and yanked the covers over my head. "Get out of that bed!" she ordered. "Er, I said get up out of that bed!" Slowly I got up, knowing I'd be punished, or at the very least, reprimanded. Instead Aunt Edna quickly led me by the hand to the crowded party room and dropped a quarter in the jukebox. "Now let me see what you got!" she said.

"In fron' a all deese people?" I asked.

"Yes, child. Don't be shame-faced. You can dance!" In pajamas, to Jackie Wilson's "Lonely Teardrops," I twisted and shuffled as her customers cheered me on. A proud Aunt Edna snapped her fingers, threw her head back, and laughed. "Errrrr! Get down to the real niddy-griddy!" From that moment on, she let me entertain her customers whenever I spent the night. At a charge of fifty cents a dance I did the "slop," the "Uncle Willie," and the "twist," sometimes earning up to five dollars for a night's work. Those weekends at Aunt Edna's place made living in our new neighborhood bearable.

After a year Mama became disgusted with conditions in Hough and, in 1963, moved us into a new apartment complex near downtown. They were nothing like the rat-infested building on LaGrange.

She Can Go Where Pretty Girls Go
───────────

Longwood Gardens were clean modern two-story units with fully equipped laundry rooms, immaculate lawns, and landscaped courtyards. Our new home had a small living-and-dining area downstairs, three bedrooms and a bath upstairs. A modern kitchenette housed brand-new appliances including a contraption in the sink called a garbage disposal. "Mama, we rich?" I asked. She smiled. Actually, the complex was just a new development for low-income families, but to me it might just as well have been Beverly Hills.

Happy with our new surroundings, Mama was also thrilled that her eldest sister Gertrude Summers had recently moved into the same complex. So was I. My favorite aunt had style. A designer wardrobe complimented her tall confident frame, and her long wavy red hair was always groomed to perfection. Mama looked up to Auntie and rarely made an important decision without first consulting with her. Considered the most prosperous of the sisters, she owned a house in the country and previously co-owned a diner with her husband Charles, a big dark-skinned man with a reserved manner, a good job at an auto plant, and an important position with the union. Auntie was also lucky playing the numbers. Her grandson Bernard, who lived with her, was a year younger than I and spoiled rotten. The recipient of a weekly allowance and any toy he desired, my cousin was quick to remind my brother, sister, and me; "Y'all poor!"

There were many reminders of how poor we were. Mama did day work (house cleaning) through an agency, but work was slow and the pay was low. She constantly complained, "I'm broker than the Ten Commandments! Got to borrow from Peter to pay Paul!" We were on "The Charity." That's what welfare was called in those days. We didn't receive money. Instead we got surplus food: mostly canned goods, powdered eggs, and instant milk. Vouchers were provided for school clothes twice a year. It was the only time we got

Up the Road

new clothes, and even then only a few items. A "case worker" dropped in randomly to make sure no man occupied our home and that our family looked as poor as was required. Despite the lack of money we felt blessed. We had been a lot poorer. But it was hard on Mama with three kids and no man.

Several months after moving into Longwood Gardens, Mama starting seeing a heavy-set soft-spoken man named Westley Wright. He moved in almost immediately. Westley seemed to like children. A talented artist, he taught us to draw, helped with our homework, and played board games with us for hours on end. Mama seemed happy. Then Westley lost his job and everything changed. They started arguing, mostly about him not looking for work. He had taken over the household chores and child supervision while Mama worked a new job as a nurse's aide. "Westley, you gotta git a job!" she yelled repeatedly to no avail. "Before I take care of some man, I rather drink muddy water and sleep in a hollow log!"

It was around that time Mama started drinking heavily. She could be frightening when drunk: yelling, cursing, and sometimes trashing the house during enraged arguments with Westley. In the middle of the night, sometimes school nights, we children would have to get out of bed and clean up. As the drinking continued, my seven-year-old sister became nervous and my eleven-year-old brother withdrew. Tall for his age, with big sad eyes like our mother, Lester was never a big talker to begin with. He began to have even less contact with the family, spending more time on the basketball court, locked in his room listening to Motown, or working his paper route. He had already won a beautiful gold bike for signing up the most customers in his district.

After a year, when Mama decided, "I jus' can't take it no damn mo!" Westley moved out and the family worked toward healing—especially my mother. She moved a new man in less than six months after Westley left. Nearly six feet tall, handsome, and a snappy dresser, Walter Thomas was also at times loud and obnoxious. He owned a large collection of guns, which I found frightening. Upset when Mama initially announced he was moving in, I strongly objected.

"Things are fine jus' the way they are!"

"No they not!" she challenged as she put out a half-smoked unfiltered Phillip Morris. "It is *hell* being broke, tryin' to raise three kids on ya own! He got a good job and I got mouths to feed." The forty-year-old truck driver for A&W Foods earned nearly three hundred dollars a week, good money in those days.

The first thing Mama's new boyfriend did was completely refurnish our house. The crippled blue couch was gone, replaced by a gold French Provincial sofa and matching chair. My proud mother had them professionally covered in plastic. "I don't wanna ketch nobody sleepin' on the new couch!" she warned, as if anyone would find sleeping on plastic comfortable. She compulsively cleaned the new marble-inlayed tables, stereo console, and floor model color television, one of the first in our neighborhood. On the wall above it hung Mama's new pictures of President John F. Kennedy and Dr. Martin Luther King Jr. There were also three new "bedroom suites." I originally shared the mid-sized bedroom with my brother, but we were getting older and feeling uncomfortable being roommates. After one too many arguments, I moved into my sister's small room. We spent weeks decorating with hand-painted pictures and artwork, appreciative of all that Walter had done.

Although generous, Walter wasn't very warm. In spite of Mama's numerous complaints, he showed little affection toward her. He was merely cordial with us children, except when he needed an audience for his long-winded, repetitive old celebrity stories. There was the half-hour "Mafia was gonna kill Sammy Davis when he messed wit that white broad, Mai Britt!" story. We ran for cover from any sentence that began with "Ava Gardner the most beautiful

Up the Road

white broad in the world!" The most boring were the old gangster stories. "I knew Elliott Ness, lived right here in Cleveland!" Walter got along best with my sister, was cordial to my brother, and didn't seem to care for me at all.

I never did understand why Walter disliked me. It was as if he was trying to drive a wedge between my mother and me. If something turned up missing, he always accused *me*. It wasn't as if I had a history of bad behavior. Sometimes it was something as petty as a missing soda. Other times it got quite serious.

When I was eleven, a gun from Walter's arsenal came up missing. He accused me in front of my mother of being the thief. "Go head and tell yo Mama the truth!" he bellowed. "What you do with my gun?"

"Troublemaker!" I yelled back. Turning to my mother I asked, "Now, what would I do wit' a gun?"

"First of all, you don't be raisin' yo voice to grown folks, fresh ass!" she shouted at me.

"But he started it!" I replied. "He's *always* starting somethin'!"

"Shuddup!" she said. "Now take yo grown ass downstairs and go do some work. I *bet* them dishes need washin'. And I bet not ketch you cuttin' yo eyes at nobody!"

"Yeah, go do some work," echoed Walter.

"And Walter, you need to stop signifying cause you don't really know *who* took the damn gun!" yelled Mama. Daily, Mama played referee to Walter's and my bickering, which usually ended with her reminding me to "Stay in a chile's place!"

Within two weeks the case of the missing gun was solved. I don't know how but Mama discovered Walter had taken the gun himself and given it to some woman. Boiling mad, she screamed, "Walter, you oughta be shame of yo damn self! Accusin' that chile a stealin' yo gun when you know you gave it to some ol' ho-ish ass bitch a yos!" He just stood there with his mouth half-open, quiet, looking guilty. Over the next year Mama gave Walter hell about that gun, especially after she'd had a couple of drinks.

While home life wasn't always exactly ideal, I loved school. My brother attended Kennard Junior High, within walking distance. My eight-year-old sister, diagnosed as farsighted and prescribed special glasses, had to attend classes for the visually impaired outside our district. Deb was too young to take the five-mile bus ride alone. Officials at John Burroughs—a regulation school with two specially equipped classrooms for students with bad to nonexistent vision—recommended that I attend the same school so I could take her back and forth. Extremely nearsighted, I had to wear glasses as well but would be attending regular classes. I was called into the principal's office my first day and assigned another eight-year-old "sight saver," an albino girl who lived en route. "Pick up your pay here every Friday after school," instructed principal Rhinehart.

"I'm getting paid?" I asked.

"Of course. Your job title is 'guide.' You'll get ten dollars per student, twenty dollars a week."

"I'm gonna be rich!" I whispered.

What I was—was extremely busy. Besides my guide job, I was elected "captain of the guard" and placed in charge of twenty-five street-crossing, door, and hall guards. I also had to maintain an A-average, something I had managed since starting school. After school, Miss Watson, my teacher and mentor for the fifth and sixth grades, privately tutored me in French and classical music appreciation. I learned to play the harpsichord as well. Not offered in school curriculums at the time, she also taught me "Negro" history. Especially fascinating were stories about the toast of Paris in the Roaring Twenties, Josephine Baker: celebrated entertainer, civil rights activist, and spy for the Allies during World War II. I was astonished to learn that the first self-made American female millionaire was a Negro named Madame C.J. Walker. During the late 1800s through early 1900s she specialized in hair and beauty products for Negro women. I passed everything I learned on to my sister. "Miss Watson said, 'being Negro, female, or different could never be an excuse for not achieving something in life. Nothing is!'"

At age eleven, puberty brought forth complications I could no longer ignore. Since age four I had realized I was different, not like my brother or other boys I knew. I was fully aware I was a boy and acted accordingly but, not knowing why, felt I should have been a girl. Raised in the rural South, I hadn't been exposed to anything except what were considered "normal" males and females. And far too young to know anything about sexuality, sex had absolutely nothing to do with it. I just knew I was a girl. Instinctively, I knew not to share my "secret" with anyone. I just prayed on it. "Since God created me, surely He understood," I thought. Instead of praying to be like other boys, I asked to be made female, even though it seemed impossible. Everyone knew that if you were born a boy or girl that was how you died.

Acting as sort of a defense mechanism, my mind had devised a way for me to cope. During the day I was Arlee and Junior as required. At nighttime I lay in bed visualizing how I felt my life should be. I gave myself the name Connie (Constance) because I felt like a Connie. Pretty, smart, and all-girl, I visualized my perception of a normal life: loving family, great friends, nice boyfriend, beautiful home, and financial stability. My nighttime family was usually from one of the popular sitcoms of the day, *The Donna Reed Show* or *Ozzie and Harriet*. I visualized every detailed scene, picking up where I left off the night before. For a few hours a night I felt complete. The "dreams" lasted from ages nine to twelve, at which point I began to try and deal with my problems in a real sense.

Gradually I began to be treated and thought of as "different" by those closest to me. Insinuations of homosexuality came from my mother and brother when I reached age twelve. Lester found it difficult to deal with my "difference," perhaps feeling betrayed that I was not the brother he wanted or needed. During fights he sometimes resorted to calling me the name I dreaded the most, "Punk! Look at how you sit!" Once he made me so mad I threw half a bowl of corn flakes at him, barely missing his head. Even though I didn't know what my condition was, I was convinced it was *not* homosexuality.

My mother told me years later, "You was diff'rent from the day you was born." When I asked how, she answered, "I don't know baby, jus' diff'rent." Mama never allowed anyone to call me names or refer to my "problem." On the other hand she gave me tips, especially on how not to sit. "Unlock yo ankles!" she constantly reminded me. I got a crash course on "how to be more masculine," including walking and speech pointers. I even received boxing lessons from my mother, which came in handy.

Our once-peaceful neighborhood had become infested with crime and in a period of three years deteriorated from family-friendly Longwood Gardens to the "New Projects," complete with street gangs. Mama felt if we were going to survive in the projects, we had to stand up for ourselves, especially me. Being fair-skinned, skinny, four-eyed, and "different" made me a waving red flag for bullies. Mama's rule of thumb for dealing with a group of thugs was: "Git the leader. The rest'll run." We were warned never to run home from a fight because "Then you gotta deal wit' me!" Hardly a week went by without some sort of confrontation. I had to fight so much I became good at it. Once, I had to defend my brother against two bully brothers. Though my brother and I weren't close, if one was threatened, the other was there. When the bullies' mother came to our house to complain, "Yo child beat my boys with a rubber hose!" Mama yelled proudly, "Yo bad-ass kids need they asses whupped!" Then she slammed the door in the woman's shocked face.

Up the Road

When all else failed in my mother's attempt to make me more masculine, she called out the big guns. The house was cleared for my counseling session with Auntie, whom Mama thought could handle *any* situation. Taking it dead serious, Auntie sat down at the dining table, folded her hands in front of her, and cleared her throat. I leafed nervously through a Halle Brothers circular my mother had left behind. "Are you funny?" Auntie asked me.

"Well, I don't know. I guess so," I answered. Sensing confusion, she tried to explain.

"A funny is a person who like the same sex."

"No, Auntie, I'm not funny," I chuckled nervously.

"You ever have sex before?" Extremely uncomfortable by then, I pretended not to hear.

"Auntie, I bet you'd look great in this," I said pointing to a powder blue dress in the circular I had been looking at during the entire conversation.

"Ooooh, that *is* pretty," said Auntie as she pulled the book closer for a better look.

"It would look great with your red hair, parted on the side, and one side pulled behind the ear."

"Get a comb and brush and show me!"

After two days of counseling no problems were solved but my aunt and I bonded. Her advice, "Baby, whatever you are, be the best," was taken to heart. "You have good taste," she added, then hired me as her hair stylist and personal shopper. Auntie entrusted me with wads of money with instructions to "Shop only at Halle Brothers, the best department store in the city."

By age thirteen I began to care less about how my family or anyone else perceived me. I concentrated on the things I enjoyed most: acting classes, which I had started at the Harris-Hardy Studio of Stage Arts, and dancing. Dancing became my passion—and I was good at it.

B.Y.O.B.

With instructions to "Bring yo butt straight home!" Mama sent me on my most dreaded chore—grocery shopping at A&P. Having to pay with newly issued government food stamps, I scanned the store before pulling out the bright dollar-sized coupons that seemed to scream, "Hey look! I'm poor!" On the way home, I was distracted, then detoured by a small crowd of sharp-dressed teenagers "jammin" to James Brown in one of the complex's many playgrounds. They did some amazing dance moves, the likes of which I had never seen. A statuesque brown-skinned girl and her partner stood out. Sporting a short mod cut and pale yellow mini, she gyrated to the record's intense drum solo. Her thin handsome partner, decked out in a slick process and sharkskin, was the best dancer I had ever seen. At one point he shook his shoulders so fast they seemed to be *shivering*. Unable to contain my enthusiasm, I set my groceries down and applauded. The pretty girl in yellow smiled at me, curtsied, then walked over.

"Hi, I'm Diane Hunter and this is my partner, Butch Mitchell," she said.

"My name is Arlee, but some people call me Junior," I replied. "Y'all got down!"

B.Y.O.B.

"Thanks," she winked. "I bet you can git down too!"

"Me?"

"Yeah, *you*! I double-dare you to show me what you got!" More than eager, I backed up, tightened my shoelaces, then danced my best to James Brown's "I Got The Feeling." Everyone applauded—Diane and Butch, the loudest.

To further test my skills, Butch did a series of steps. "Try that!" he challenged. I did, adding a few steps of my own. He looked at me and slowly nodded his head. "Excuse us for a second," he said. Then he and Diane stepped away for a private discussion, obviously about me.

When they returned, Diane said, "I'd like my mother and sister to see you dance. I live right over there." She pointed to a nearby complex. At her house, another round of applause was followed by a second conference. This time Diane's mother and sister were included. I waited patiently on the sofa, taking in compliments from kids who had followed us in from the playground. After their brief meeting, Diane finally let me in on what they had been discussing. "Me and Butch are a professional dance team. We perform at cabarets and special events all over the city. My mother's our manager and chaperone, my sister our advisor and costume designer—and you? You the *baddest* ass dancer we've ever seen! Give me five!" Her hand swung down and met mine in a loud stinging slap. "We want you in our group," she smiled.

"Yeah, We'd be the toughest mothafuckas in town!" Butch added. I was speechless!

"These cool dancers want me?" I thought.

I quickly regained my ability to speak when told "The pay's a hundred dollars a night—each." Cabaret season was from September to April of the following year. We would have to perform two nights a week, two shows a night.

"Yes, yes, yes!"

She Can Go Where Pretty Girls Go

Mama was furious when I finally arrived home, two hours late with the groceries. "Where the hell you been boy?" she hollered. I thought somethin' had happened! Oughta use yo head for mo sides a hat rack!" Carefully, I tried explaining.

"Mama, I was dancing. I met these really nice people named Diane and Butch and they want me to join their dance group."

"Dance group? Dance group? Where you spose to be dancin' chile?"

"Cabaret parties," I replied hesitantly.

"Ca—ca—cabaret?" she frowned. "Cabarets for *grown* folk and they serve liquor. You only *thirteen*, boy!"

"Mama, *please*! Diane's mother'll be chaperoning and I'll come home right after our show. And besides, we're getting a hundred dollars a night—each!" With that revelation came permission.

At my first meeting at Diane's, there were a house full of teenagers, all vocalizing their opinions and concepts for the new group. Butch, at eighteen, was the oldest and coolest. With everyone in agreement, he insisted I needed a new image. "Grow your hair out! Lose the bookworm glasses! Get a cooler wardrobe!" Diane taught me how to smoke king-sized Kools, the in cigarette for the urban black teen. At six feet tall with the body of a full-grown woman, I was shocked when I found out she was my age, thirteen! Even more shocking, teenagers were allowed to drink and smoke at her house, something my mother would never allow. The only adult in the house was Diane's mother/manager/chaperone Gloria "Tootsie" Hunter, a pleasant short, heavy-set woman with an unkempt "natural," who stayed glued to her armchair dispensing advice and critiques. Our biggest critic was Diane's fifteen-year-old sister and our costume designer Anita, who also had a crush on me. Her sixteen-year-old boyfriend Anthony Baker somewhat resented me—not because of the crush—because he had expected to be chosen as third member of the dance group.

B.Y.O.B.

A strong, ambitious dancer, he had won several competitions with his unofficial partner Tonya Roberts, a fifteen-year-old copper-skinned beauty who sometimes served as a fourth member of our troupe. The rest of the main group included: our self appointed bodyguard, seventeen-year-old Tyrone, eleven-year-old aspiring dancer Chico who ran errands for our troupe, Diane's boyfriend Winifred, Butch's girlfriend Diane Harper, and Tanya's best friend, Denise. They were all present at every rehearsal.

Rehearsals were long, five to six hours a day, four days a week. My partners and I shared the responsibility of choreographing routines, which were fast-paced and sometimes acrobatic. At five-feet-six and only a hundred and eighteen pounds, I had to lift Diane, who said she was one hundred and thirty pounds (I think she might have lied). Besides learning the routines, each of us was required to have a "specialty" step for our solos. And it had to be something extraordinary, guaranteed to bring the house down. Diane's was her sexy bumps and grinds. "I can do a whole lot of damage with these hips," she boasted, before treating me to a sample. Butch had his shoulder shiver.

"I do whatever the music tells me but I always end with my moneymaker," he said. What you gonna do, Junior? I know it's gonna be cool."

"I'm still working on it, but it'll be ready by show time," I promised, not yet ready to unveil my masterpiece. I had been practicing day and night.

My debut performance was on September 20, 1966, at a popular black nightspot called The Red Carpet. With over five hundred in attendance, a live band "jammed" hot soul sounds as couples packed the floor. Cabarets were B.Y.O.B. (Bring Your Own Bottle) parties, and people did—by the bags and boxes. Our entourage of over thirty: our manager, her friends, and the gang occupied two long tables directly in front.

My partners and I had to share a dressing room, but it was large with floor-to-ceiling mirrors and a private bath. Butch and I changed into our print dashikis and white narrow legged pants. Wearing *her* dashiki as a micro-mini, Diane added matching panties, sure to be exposed during her provocative solo. Tootsie came backstage to check on us and bring Butch and Diane a bottle of 151-proof rum and a Coke. "We have a couple of sips just before the show to ease the nerves," said Diane. She poured me one. "For ya nerves," she whispered.

"Oh, no thanks," I said.

"For ya *nerves*!" she repeated slightly louder. After drinking too much, too fast, and gagging, I did feel more relaxed—but my throat felt like it was on *fire*! I had never even tasted liquor before, but had seen its adverse effects on my mother and her friends. Excited and nervous, I was more concerned about getting through my debut than with the negatives of alcohol.

With the band playing in the background, the master of ceremonies introduced us. "Ladies and gentlemen! Put your hands together for the baaadest dance group in Cleveland! Diane! Butch! and Arleeee!" The band exploded with Archie Bell and The Drell's "Tighten Up" as we came out single file, "tightnin' up" low-down and funky. Our energy was phenomenal and the audience felt it. They screamed and applauded as we performed our opening routine to perfection. Butch was the first to solo. He did an incredibly fast spin toward front-center stage, ending in a full split. To yells of "Do yo thang!" he slowly rose, rotating his hips. Women were jumping and screaming. Then suddenly, to their absolute joy, he pulled two onstage and nasty-danced with them. Ending with his "shoulder shake," Butch was given a standing ovation.

As Butch joined me in the background, Diane shook her way to center stage then teased with her raunchy bumps and grinds. "Sock it to me, baby!" one man hooted. "Shake it, don't break it!"

hollered another. Seductive and hard, she rolled her hips with almost every step she took—and the men loved it! I thought they were going to rush the stage when, naughtily smiling, Diane jumped and landed in a half-split, her panties fully exposed. Finishing with a series of gyrations, she was rewarded with a howling ovation.

Then came my turn. After traveling the length of the large stage, spinning and grinding in triple time, I did a daring jump-kick that ended in a split. I followed with an impossible back lean. Popping my hips from side to side, in perfect balance I slowly leaned backwards until my swaying shoulders brushed the floor. "Gone baby! Git down wit' yo bad self!" the audience cheered. I ended the fifteen-minute solo with the unveiling of my special step. Not even Butch and Diane had seen it.

First my stomach started vibrating, followed by my chest and legs. Soon every muscle in my body vibrated—at a speed that looked more mechanical than human. I leaned backwards, shivering my way down to the floor and back up again. Then I shivered my way across the stage, into the audience, and back. Everyone went wild, including Butch and Diane, who were jumping and "slapping each other five." People threw money at my feet, which our manager Tootsie quickly retrieved. They were still cheering as I shivered upstage for our synchronized closing routine. As we danced our way off, people were still applauding—and Tootsie was still picking up money.

Backstage, Diane kissed me on the lips and Butch lifted me off the floor and spun me around. "Yo ass is bad and we gonna make a lotta money!" he shouted. "How the hell you make yo body shake like that?"

"I call it the shiver," I said proudly, "inspired by your shoulder shake."

"Really? But my step can't compare to yours," said Butch as he attempted the shiver. "*Yours* is impossible to do! Let's see what you can do in the second show."

She Can Go Where Pretty Girls Go

Our second show was even hotter. Three encores were celebrated with a toast backstage. My second drink. Tootsie collected our money from the cabaret sponsor and paid each of us a hundred dollars. "You guys earned it!" she said. You had everyone right in the palm of your hands. And Junior, you were great!"

"Oh, thanks," I said. The first time I held that much cash, I just stared at it, grinning. Our manager also secured four bookings for us that night. I felt like a star. That evening was, without doubt, the most exciting experience of my thirteen-year-old life.

Through dancing I was being exposed to many exciting new experiences. One came on a day in early 1967 when Diane phoned, excited, talking fast. "My mom knows this dude who works with Duke Ellington, the famous jazz musician! We're invited to his concert tonight and there might be a spot for us in the show! Isn't that great?"

"Well yeah. That's fantastic!" I replied. "But what are we suppose to do? Will we get a chance to rehearse with a band?"

"I don't know. Details are kind of sketchy but be at my house in an hour and we'll figure it out." I was of course thrilled about going to my first big concert and overwhelmed at the possibility of performing in Duke Ellington's show. But I was confused as to why a soul dance group would be asked to perform in a jazz concert.

There were three tickets waiting for us at Cleveland Music Hall. We were met by a representative of Mr. Ellington's and escorted backstage where we were informed that our troupe would not be performing after all. I don't remember the reason, but I was relieved. Everything was so last minute. Free to relax and enjoy the concert, we were escorted by Ellington's aide to some of the best seats in the house. He also invited us to an after-party being held in Mr. Ellington's hotel suite.

The house lights dimmed as the orchestra played the intro to "Take The A Train." Although that song and "Satin Doll" were two of only a few Ellington tunes I was familiar with, I was blown away. And having discovered the genius in books and old movies, it was an honor to actually see and hear him live. After the concert, Butch, Diane, and I hurried backstage to meet the legend. With his straight black hair pulled back in a neat ponytail and large bags under his eyes, he looked a lot older than I had expected. "Thank you for coming," he smiled as he shook our hands.

"Thank *you*!" said Diane. "We enjoyed every moment."

"It was fantastic!" I smiled.

"Yeah, y'all got down!" said Butch. We were then given Ellington's suite number at the hotel located just across the street.

There were about fifty people at the party. Cultured and elegantly dressed, they were different from the adults I was accustomed to. Mr. Ellington's aide introduced Diane, Butch, and me as a well-known local dance group, which made me feel proud. Shortly after our arrival, Duke Ellington walked in. He spoke briefly with some of his guests then walked over to a beautiful white grand piano and sat down. It appeared we were going to be treated to an impromptu concert. I managed to get a good spot, standing right next to the piano. When Mr. Ellington invited me to sit on the bench with him, Diane, standing nearby, handed me a glass of champagne. I tried to act sophisticated but was about to burst. There I was: a thirteen-year-old kid living in the projects, sipping champagne, and sitting next to the great Duke Ellington as he played a medley of his legendary music. "Miss Watson [my fifth and sixth grade teacher] would be so proud of me," I thought. She had been the one who introduced me to the composer's life and music.

After the performance, I shook Mr. Ellington's hand and he wished Diane, Butch, and me "The best of luck with your dancing." I couldn't wait to get home and tell my sister about my extraordinary evening.

I did my best to look after my ten-year-old sister. For a period, Mama and her boyfriend Walter partied on the weekends. They hosted card games or went out. Deb was too young to stay home alone so I often took her along when I performed. I put her long hair up in a French roll, applied a little makeup, and dressed her older. My manager and her friends looked after her while I danced and she was taken home immediately following the last show. Deb loved it. We would laugh and talk half the night about what happened at the cabarets.

While dancing at cabarets was becoming my entire world, my interest in school was waning. Whereas elementary school had been nurturing, I was pretty much on my own at Kennard Junior High. Placed in the school's college prep classes, called Section A, I was extremely unpopular. Only a few students had heard about my dancing. To the majority I was just a bookworm, a "square." But that was about to change.

Diane and I were both fourteen and in the ninth grade when she transferred from Hamilton to Kennard. She was placed in Section A as well and we took most of our classes together. Hip, and the best-dressed girl in school, all the cool kids wanted to hang with Diane who was surprised by my unpopularity. "I feel comfortable and act differently around you and our friends," I confided in her.

"It's time you showed these kids," said Diane. "That you're hipper than all of them put together!"

One day Diane asked me to go to "rec," a dance held in the school gym and lunchtime hangout for the super hip. Intimidated, I said "No!"

"Junior, I am not taking *no* for an answer," she said. "Now come on, let's go! *Please?*"

"Okay, but I'm not dancing!"

As soon as we got there, she insisted, "Come on Junior, let's dance!"

"I don't feel like it!" I half-whined. She completely ignored me and walked straight over to the student in charge of spinning records to request a song. Abruptly, the record playing was cut short to make way for James Brown's "I Got the Feeling". Diane grabbed my hand, pulled me to the center of the dance floor, and started dancing—hard!

"Four corners!" she shouted. "Come on now Junior, hit it!" Knowing she wouldn't be satisfied until I gave it my all, I finally gave in and started dancing like I was getting paid. Everyone else stopped dancing and encircled us. "Shiver!" yelled Diane. "Shiverrrr!"

By the time I did the shiver the entire gym was chanting, "Go, Arlee, go!" After our dance everyone applauded and crowded around. Guys patted me on the back: girls asked to dance with me. Diane just stood back and smiled slyly. She had made her point.

After that day in "rec" the school in-crowd started acting differently toward me, speaking in the hallways and inviting me to sit at their tables during lunch. I wasn't interested. Diane and I were more into planning new outfits or rehearsing new dance steps for upcoming shows. Besides, I realized that it wasn't as important what people thought about me as what I thought about myself. With Diane's encouragement, my confidence was soaring.

After over two years dancing on the cabaret circuit I began to long for something new. I got tired of the same old raunchy routines, and it wasn't the same after Butch got drafted into the Army and Diane and I became a duo. To Diane's dismay, I decided to quit the group. It was one of the most difficult things I had ever done. Though we phoned periodically, I saw little of Diane and the gang afterwards. She continued dancing, with Anthony Baker as her new partner. I had to find *my* niche. It was 1967 and things were changing. So was I.

The "Black Power Movement" marched through my neighborhood just as it had throughout most cities in black America. Blacks embraced their African heritage and gained a newfound sense of pride. Many changed their "slave" names to African names and took to wearing dashikis. We all began calling ourselves black and considered "Negro" or "colored" insulting, grounds for confrontation.

The Honorable Elijah Muhammad headed the Black Muslims who spoke out vehemently against America's racial injustices. Malcolm X broke from the group to become one of the Black Movement's most respected leaders. Having been successful in bringing the issue of racial segregation and injustices to the forefront through his nonviolent philosophy, Rev. Dr. Martin Luther King, Jr. was revered. We became united under his leadership. My mother and sister got a chance to see and hear the great civil rights leader at the Longwood Plaza, three blocks from our home. I had to rehearse for an upcoming dance contest and missed the event. Deb was so excited about seeing Dr. King in person she talked all evening about it. "His voice was so powerful he gave me goose bumps! He made me feel so proud to be black!" Regretful at missing the historic event, I promised myself the next time the dynamic leader spoke in my neighborhood I would go to see him, no matter what.

Whereas 1967 was a year of hopes and dreams, 1968 became a year of losses of tragic proportions. My family and I were watching television when our program was interrupted by a special news bulletin. "Dr. Martin Luther King, Jr. has just been assassinated outside his hotel room in Memphis, Tennessee!" Numbed, my entire family wept; even my mother's boyfriend Walter; who I had never seen shed a tear. "That's a goddamn shame," he said. "Why the hell they have to go and *kill* em!" Mom nearly fainted. Tearful neighbors dropped by and calls from family and friends poured in as black America mourned the loss of its greatest and most beloved leader. We all tried to make sense of the tragedy but, of course, no one could. All we felt was a deep dark sense of irreplaceable loss and anger. King's assassination dealt a crippling blow to the Black Movement.

Senator Robert Kennedy was also assassinated in 1968 while campaigning for the United States presidency. America hadn't fully recovered from the assassination of his brother, John F. Kennedy, during his presidency five years earlier. Robert Kennedy championed black causes and we were exceedingly optimistic about his run. His death was taken extremely hard. It seemed that anyone who fought for human rights for black people would end up assassinated.

Nineteen sixty-eight became a year of racial upheaval. There were riots in Newark, New Jersey, Detroit, Michigan, and the Glenville area of Cleveland. The evening news showed businesses and communities on fire, looting, and blacks battling with the National Guard. It was a repeat of the Watts (Los Angeles) riots of 1965, the year Malcolm X was assassinated. The riots eventually came to our front door. Longwood Gardens shut itself in for two days while stores, businesses, our community—burned!

With so much going on, dancing seemed trivial. After leaving the cabaret circuit, the only performing I had done was for an auto show. I stopped dancing altogether for a while, needing time to figure things out and chart my next move.

UPBEAT!

$\mathcal{I}$n August of 1968 the *Cleveland Plain Dealer* announced that *Upbeat* was holding auditions for new dancers. Teens from ages fifteen to eighteen had a shot at becoming a regular on the popular weekly-televised show. Nationally syndicated in over a hundred cities, it featured top contemporary recording stars of the sixties. Simon and Garfunkel made their very first television appearance on the show. Rock super-groups Three Dog Night, Steppenwolf, Iron Butterfly, the Yardbirds, and Eric Burdin and the Animals were guests. Singers John Denver, Kenny Rogers, and Neil Sedaka also appeared along with top names from Motown: Smokey Robinson and The Miracles, The Temptations, Stevie Wonder, The Four Tops. Other guests included The O Jays, The Impressions with Curtis Mayfield, Little Anthony and The Imperials, Sly and The Family Stone, The Fifth Dimension, BB King, Little Richard, and Johnny Mathis. The great Otis Redding performed his hit, "Try a Little Tenderness" on the show in 1967. According to Upbeat archives, afterwards he performed live at Leo's Casino, a popular nightspot featuring the top names in soul. Redding left Cleveland by plane that night, headed for Wisconsin. He never made it. The plane crashed, killing him and most of his band. Sadly, *Upbeat* was Otis Redding's last television appearance.

The "*Upbeat* Dancers" appeared frequently throughout the hour-long show dancing alongside an array of stars lip-synching their latest hit. Often opening and closing the show, the dancers had a featured routine as well. It was every teen's dream to dance on a show like *Upbeat*—including mine. I only told my sister I was auditioning. "Deb, do you really think I have a chance?" I asked.

"Pa—*leaze*," she replied rolling her eyes. "You're better than every last dancer on that show, and you know it."

Held at the WEWS television station on Thirty-seventh and Euclid, the audition was swarmed with hundreds of attractive, hyper energetic teens. The anxious mob filled the wooden bleachers in Studio C and the waiting area just outside. There was an air of excitement in the room. Several teens practiced. Others talked or sat nervously waiting for their big chance. *Upbeat* house band People's Choice set up while the show's staff rushed to pass out questionnaire forms and "number" each dancer. Numbers were written on sheets of white paper in black marker and pinned onto the backs of all the dancers' clothing. Mine was 35.

Being inside a television studio for the first time was an experience in itself. The size of a school gym, it seemed much bigger on television. From the high ceiling hung elaborate lighting equipment. A glass-enclosed control room, situated high above the floor, gave the director an overall view. Two large television cameras stood idle at the far end of the studio among piles of thick black cables. Along one wall were retractable wooden bleachers where the studio audience sat during tapings. That was where I sat, squeezed in among countless other hopefuls. Seated to my left was a slim, sophisticated-looking black girl with an engaging smile and big "outta sight" afro. "Hi, I'm Gail Philpott. I go to Glenville. What school do you go to?" she asked.

She Can Go Where Pretty Girls Go

"East Tech," I replied.

"Numbers one through twenty!" a voice rang out, signaling the start of auditions.

"There're sure a lot of people trying out," Gail remarked, scanning the studio, sizing up the competition. "Nervous?"

"A little," I confessed, half-paying attention. My focus was on the first group of competitors on the floor, nervously ready. On the band's first pounding beats, they erupted into their best routine. Some danced so hard limbs seemed ready to pop from their sockets. One tall skinny white boy flipped into a perfect Chinese split while his bouncy blonde partner wowed us with her double-jointed "four corners." Included in the next group auditioning, I began to get anxious as the band neared the end of their number.

"Break a leg!" smiled Gail—not exactly the words I wanted to hear right before dancing.

By the time "Number thirty-five!" was yelled out I was already on the floor, standing directly in front of the judges. The biggest show smile I could conjure flashed across my face when the band started playing "Tighten Up," a song I had performed to a thousand times. An upbeat tempo, driving bass line, and "super bad" drum solo made it my favorite—and my body knew every single beat. I twisted and rolled into my best steps with maximum energy and graceful ease. After a few "bumps and grinds"—just to let the judges know I could—I danced with every girl on the floor doing a different dance with each: the Hip City, the Philly Dog, the African Twist, the funky Four Corners. When the drummer began his loud hypnotic solo I became entranced. Controlled by the volume and speed of the beats, my body gradually moved from a slow smooth shake to a fast tremble to the vibratory state that I called the shiver. Dancers in the bleachers stood and cheered as others rushed the floor for a better view. My body vibrated even faster as I danced across the floor, playing to the judges with the

Upbeat!

biggest smile I could muster. Then, as abruptly as it started, the music stopped. Some applauded as I left the floor. And when I returned to my seat, an excited Gail grabbed me. "You got down! You got down!" Having done my personal best, I was confident I had delivered a perfect audition. Dancing before the brutally critical cabaret audiences had made me a seasoned performer.

There were several "dance-offs." If your number was skipped over when dancers were called to the floor, it meant you were eliminated. Relieved whenever mine was called, I danced each time as if my life depended on it. Finally, after several hours and hundreds of cuts, a gentleman from *Upbeat* announced, "We have chosen eight dancers!" The studio silenced. "I want to thank everyone for participating," he said before shouting out the numbers of the lucky eight. "Number twenty-three! Number thirty-five!"

"Thirty-five? That's me!" I blurted out as he continued calling out the winning numbers. I jumped up from my seat and rushed to the floor, fighting to keep my composure during the highest moment of my life. I was also happy for the girl seated next to me. Gail Philpott's smooth soulful dance style and cute black-teen image made her a winner as well.

"Can you believe it? We're *Upbeat* Dancers!" Gail shrilled, gripping my hand.

"No! It's pretty unbelievable," I replied.

"Oh, I *knew* you were going to make it," she said, both hands on her hips. "I was shocked when you first took to the floor. Came in all quiet and shy, then get on the floor and dance your little butt off." We laughed. After quickly congratulating the other winners, I left, eager to tell my family the good news. While walking home, trying to let everything sink in, I kept repeating, "I'm going to be on television!" It blew my mind!

An article on the auditions appeared in the newspaper the following morning, stating that only eight were chosen out of eight

She Can Go Where Pretty Girls Go

hundred. The paper listed our names. Almost as excited as I was, my mother read the article aloud to the entire family, still recovering from the shock that I was going to be on television every week. Then she hugged me. "That's real nice baby. Maybe you'll be able to buy ya Mama a house," she joked. Her boyfriend Walter shook my hand.

"That's pretty good, boy," he said.

Always supportive, with a nod Deb said, "See? I told you." My brother Lester asked a million questions.

"Y'all git paid? How much you git paid? They pay y'all ev'ry week?"

My first day at *Upbeat* started with a brief orientation. Maurice "Hank" Nystrom—in his mid thirties, about five-seven and blond, with an endless supply of energy and cheer—introduced himself as the show's new choreographer. Looking the dancers over like a general inspecting his troops, he commanded, "Things are going to be done differently than they have been under the previous choreographer!" We're going to be professional!" He smiled. "The *Upbeat* Dancers are looked up to by teens across America and we have an image to uphold. Also, this is a family show and there will be no on-camera bumps and grinds." He glanced in my direction. Dating the stars was "absolutely prohibited!" Most of the entertainers were adult males and the average age of the dancers was sixteen. Extremely protective, the show kept tabs on the dancers. What they did *outside* the studio was just as important as what happened *inside* Studio C. If someone's conduct came into question, the choreographer got a call from producer Herman Spero, associate producer Walter Maskey, or his secretary Shirley. The dancer then received a call from Hank demanding that any problem be "handled immediately!" It usually was.

Rehearsals were Tuesday and Thursday evenings and lasted two hours. Tapings were Saturdays, from 9:00 a.m. until 4:00 p.m.

Upbeat!

and the show aired on Saturdays at 5:00 p.m. The weekly pay for a "principal" was twenty dollars per routine, ridiculously low considering the show's success. The principals or "regulars" were the nine or ten dancers who actually appeared on camera each week. The remaining dancers were called "clappers." Though required to be at rehearsals, learn routines, and attend Saturday tapings, they rarely appeared on camera. A clapper was only paid five dollars a week and mostly sat with the studio audience during tapings, helping to provide the applause and energy needed for the show.

My first rehearsal felt like another audition. Hank announced, "Only nine will be used in the routine this coming Saturday. Whoever learns the steps *first* and does them the *best* will be chosen." You had to be "on your toes" to keep up with Hank. He only demonstrated a step twice and was on to the next. Eight were chosen rather quickly: four white girls, two black girls, and two white boys. Nine were needed for the routine, leaving only one spot open.

The principal black male dancer was a handsome and friendly seventeen-year-old suburbanite named Billy Davis, a six-month veteran with the show. The last opening in the lineup was usually his, but I did so well learning the steps Hank thought it only fair that he and I compete for the spot. I knew it was more than just a dance-off to appear in that week's routine. Whoever won the competition would be the principal dancer for *all* the routines. I felt sorry for Billy.

Hank ordered everyone off the floor but Billy and me. Then he put on a forty-five and counted down, "And five, six, seven, eight!" Unable to afford a single slip-up, I had every step down pat. My competitor didn't fare so well keeping up with the fast-paced choreography. Continuously forgetting the sequence, he resorted to watching my feet in a hopelessly desperate attempt to

She Can Go Where Pretty Girls Go

refresh his memory. Even before the competition ended, both of us knew I would be his replacement. "I'm sorry, Billy," said Hank. "I have no choice but to use Arlee in the routine." A good sport, Billy shook my hand.

"Congratulations, you're good," he said.

"Thanks, so are you," I replied. Though happy enough to shout, I maintained my cool. But it was official! I was a principal *Upbeat* Dancer and the happiest kid alive!

The WEWS television station was frenzied with excitement on Saturday, the day of my first *Upbeat* taping. Famous and soon-to-be famous rock, pop, and soul stars and their entourages mingled, waiting for direction. Dancers rehearsed. Magically transforming Studio C into the *Upbeat* show, a production team rushed to put up elaborate sets. Huge paisley cutouts were placed behind three platforms varying in height and shape. A "psychedelic" backdrop decorated an enormous round Plexiglas platform that lit up.

From nine in the morning until noon there was a complete run-through so the show's director Albert Herrick could check for sound, lighting, and camera angles. For lunch everyone headed across the street to the Versaille Hotel. By the time we returned for the one o'clock taping the studio audience had arrived and were being seated. *Upbeat* taped before a live audience of screaming diehard fans who knew all the dancers by name and collected the autographs of every star who appeared on the show.

The dancers headed straight into wardrobe. We shared the small dressing rooms with the guest stars. Of all the acts, the hard and acid rock bands wore the wildest clothes. Sheer electric floral shirts were shamelessly teamed with tight, striped hip-hugger bell-bottoms. I was hopeful for something equally as exciting. But unfortunately, clothes for the new dancers hadn't arrived yet and I was stuck with Billy Davis's old outfits, which were two sizes too large. Even though the problem was solved with safety pins

Upbeat!

---

and attitude, the blue jersey turtleneck and plain black pants fell short of what I had expected for my television debut. There were three dance numbers and my two other outfits weren't much better. I was displeased with my wardrobe but *loved* my face after ten minutes with Harvey Holocker, in-house makeup artist. I had a bad case of teen acne but in his talented hands, it was undetectable.

My heart pounded as the show's host stood on set, ready to introduce us. In his mid to late twenties, dark-haired, and wholesomely handsome, Don Webster rehearsed his lines, written on cue cards and held a few feet in front of him by sixteen-year-old David Spero, the producer's son. The dancers hurried to their starting positions. At eighteen, six-foot blond John Magill was the eldest and the choreographer's right-hand man. His partner was serious and classy longhaired blonde Linda Mulcahey. Also blonde, Beverly "Bev" Jones was one of the show's hardest workers and her partner Jimmie "Jim" Stallard, the best white dancer I had ever seen. To my delight, Gail Philpott became my partner. Dancing solo were: a pony-tailed black beauty with captivating green eyes named Arline Burks, affluent and golden-haired Jean Hagedorn, and a seventeen-year-old black cutie named Denise.

"Five minutes!" shouted our choreographer. Facing the girls, motionless in their starting positions, I stood frozen between John and Jim under hot bright lights on a set designed especially for our routine. Sensing my nervousness, six-month veteran Jim whispered, "Good luck, Arlee." Hank positioned himself in front of us just outside the camera shot to "direct" his choreography. As a Clearasil commercial showing on the studio monitors came to an end, two large cameras a few feet in front of the dancers stood ready. One of three cameramen, Jerry Gates positioned his hand for the countdown, his raised five fingers to signal the number of seconds left before the cameras rolled.

She Can Go Where Pretty Girls Go

When the red light flashed on, everyone was silent as Don Webster started our intro: "Here are the *Upbeat* Dancers now as they demonstrate the very latest in dance routines." Even though I had practiced a thousand times and could do the routine in my sleep, I was nervous. No retake if a step was flubbed, it would be seen by the entire viewing audience and preserved on tape for all eternity. The band started playing Archie Bell and The Drell's "I Just Can't Stop Dancing" and, armed with over enthusiasm and big perfect smiles, we began. My biggest concern was an upcoming lift Hank called the "plunger." Though my partner Gail was thin and light, in heels she was three inches taller than I was. When she straddled me I dipped; swung her from hip to hip, dipped again, flung her around my back then gently tossed her upward. She touched down on the eighth count and we continued the routine, right on beat. The entire routine went perfectly, not one mistake. Though undoubtedly my most exciting moment, I was relieved when my debut was over. The audience cheered and it was on to the next act. I couldn't *wait* for my family and friends to see me on television.

After that television appearance, life totally changed. I became an instant celebrity, especially popular with black teens. Family and friends called to congratulate me, including my old cabaret partner Diane. My father, who I hadn't seen or heard from since age nine even called from Washington, D.C., where he was living at the time. He said he had seen me on television and proud, mailed me twenty dollars. It was the last time I heard from him but I was happy he at least got a chance to see me dance. It seemed everyone else had. I couldn't venture outside without people yelling out, "Hey, *Upbeat!*" It blew me away the first time someone asked for my autograph outside the studio. A small group of giggling teenyboppers approached me as I shopped at a downtown store. "You look as nice as you do on TV," one giggled.

Upbeat!

Besides being recognized on the street, being an Upbeat Dancer afforded numerous opportunities and perks, including concert bookings, commercials, personal appearances, and VIP treatment at restaurants, stores, and nightclubs. We appeared frequently in the newspapers. Rock critic Jane Scott wrote a column for the *Cleveland Plain Dealer* and regularly visited the *Upbeat* set looking for her next story. She did numerous features on the dancers, demonstrating the latest moves. I was especially pleased when a caricature of me appeared on the cover of the TV guide. U-P-B-E-A-T was spelled out in large jumbled letters with my likeness dancing atop the U. Now *that* was groovy!

I also got the chance to meet and work with a galaxy of the world's most famous stars. My favorites were the soul artists. When beautiful, curvaceous Freda Payne performed her smash number-one hit, "Band of Gold," I danced alongside her. I was delighted the first time I met Stevie Wonder. Hank introduced me to him as "the other Stevie Wonder," which of course confused the singer. Stevie smiled and firmly shook my hand after my choreographer told him my *real* name and explained the initial introduction. Wonder had been scheduled to appear on an earlier show but something came up and he didn't show. The director decided to go ahead with the spot, using a previously aired tape. Needing to add some new footage, they asked me to stand in for the Motown star. My bobbing lip-synching silhouette and distant profile was edited in with footage of the real Stevie Wonder. The clip ran several times, and no one ever noticed that *one* of the Stevies was a fake.

Working with singer Rufus Thomas was also an unforgettable experience—a psychic experience. One Friday night I dreamt he was on Upbeat performing his hit, "Funky Chicken," atop a warmly lit Plexiglas riser with me dancing next to him. I woke up wondering, "Why in the world did I have such a crazy dream? I don't even like the funky chicken!" To my surprise, when I walked into

She Can Go Where Pretty Girls Go

the studio that morning for taping, there was Rufus Thomas in all his glory, rehearsing his "Funky Chicken" number.

"Arlee, dance on the riser next to Rufus," Hank instructed.

"What did you say?" I asked, just to make sure he said what I thought he said.

"On the riser, Arlee," he repeated. When we actually taped, my choreographer had me wear the exact same outfit I had on in the dream. It was bizarre watching the segment when it aired because it was exactly the way it appeared in my dream—but it looked fantastic.

One of the wilder groups to appear on *Upbeat* were the Funkadelics, headed by George Clinton. With a hot new genre of soul branded "funk," the group shocked everyone when they appeared on set to rehearse "Git Yourself Together" dressed only in diapers. Gyrating as funky as their hard-driving sound, the large nearly visible bulges in their diapers flopped about. The show's director let the group finish the run-through, then informed them, "*Upbeat* is a family show!" and that they would not be allowed to perform until appropriately dressed. After a minor protest the group changed into less distracting suede-fringed vests, ultra skin-tight pants (still no underwear), floppy hats, and long flowing scarves. The Funkadelics had a party later that evening at their Versaille Hotel suite. A couple of the girl dancers got in trouble for attending. I went, but knowing full well the show would find out, only stayed a hot minute.

I was overjoyed when I heard the "Godfather of Soul" was appearing on our show. One of the hottest recording artists in the business, James Brown's "Say It Loud, I'm Black and I'm Proud" became an anthem for young Black America. I was especially excited about the prospect of dancing on camera with "soul brother number one." But unfortunately that wasn't to be. When I arrived for taping, one of the dancers said that the show thought Brown's song of black pride too controversial for their audience. Consequently, the singer

48

wouldn't appear if he couldn't perform his hit. I was disappointed in the show if that was really their stance and upset because I wouldn't be working with the great James Brown. I refused to be cheated out of at least *meeting* him.

Through the WEWS-TV grapevine, I heard that Brown was scheduled to appear on the *Ken Hawkins Show*, taped Saturday evening in the same studio as *Upbeat*. A new black-oriented music-and-dance show that only broadcast locally in a 1:00 a.m. time slot, it showcased some of the best soul singers of the day. The show also had some "fly" dancers. Right after getting in from taping *Upbeat* I phoned the station to find out what time *Ken Hawkins* started taping. After showering and eating I rushed right back to the station. As soon as I walked into the studio, some of the "Ken Hawkins Dancers" bombarded me. My favorite, Aaron said, "I watch you every week. You know, the two best dancers in the city should work together."

"We'll talk," I said. My self-appointed host introduced me to the other dancers. Then James Brown walked in and everyone got excited—especially two female dancers who I was certain were going to burst into tears any moment. After a quick run-through Brown performed "Say It Loud, I'm Black and I'm Proud" and got the entire studio dancing. Afterwards, he graciously talked with everyone and signed autographs. It was a blast—for me, one of the highlights of 1970.

In 1970 Richard Nixon was our country's president and the Vietnam War waged on in spite of nationwide protest. As the music scene changed songs became harder edged with lyrics that protested political, social, and racial injustices. The Beetles split up and rock icons Janis Joplin and Jimi Hendrix died from drug overdoses. The voting age dropped from twenty-one to eighteen. Things were changing and so was I.

Almost seventeen, I felt completely missing. I wasn't doing too well in school. I was cutting classes and constantly in the principal's

She Can Go Where Pretty Girls Go

office, a few times for fighting. Although most thought it was cool that I danced on television, a few of the guys seemed jealous of the attention the girls were paying me and sometimes picked fights. There were always fights at East Technical High, which was becoming like a battle zone. I had already lost two classmates to gunfights on the school's front steps. When my mother refused my request for a transfer to "a better school," with great regret I dropped out in my sophomore year. I kept it a secret from the show, knowing they'd strongly disapprove.

No longer in school, *Upbeat* became everything to me. Most of my time was spent with the dancers, especially a dynamic duo named Bev Jones and Jim Stallard. We hung together so much we were being called the "Mod Squad" after a television series that introduced its three hip young cops as "One white, one black, and one blonde!" Blonde, bubbly, and cute—and a good strong dancer—high school senior Bev was also lead vocalist with a local band. Kent State freshman Jim was all-American good-looking and conservative in manner and dress—but danced with the soul of a brother. He and Bev had met four years earlier when, while delivering newspapers, he discovered her dancing on the front porch. They starting dating, became dance partners, and later won spots on *Upbeat*. Against Bev's wishes, when Jim went away to school he broke off the relationship, deciding they were best as friends and dance partners.

Whenever Jim came home from school, usually on Tuesdays, Thursdays, and weekends, we'd hang out, talk on the phone, or he and Bev would visit me. I wasn't welcome in Jim's home. His parents hated black people. One evening, as we were talking on the phone, I heard his mom yell in the background, "You still on the phone with that nigger?"

Flabbergasted, I demanded, "Jim, let me speak with her!"

"Now Arlee, pay no attention to that," he pleaded.

"No, put-her-on-the-phone!" I said. Surprisingly, he did.

As I struggled to remain calm, I said, "Mrs. Stallard, you should be ashamed of yourself for being so hateful. If 'that word' ever escapes from your mouth again, you *will* be receiving a personal visit!" She never let me hear her use the "n" word again, although I'm sure it remained a part of her vocabulary.

Tired of the grueling drives back and forth from Kent State, Jim stopped coming home, except for the occasional weekend. I didn't see him much but we stayed in touch, writing and calling whenever we could. One day he phoned in a panic, a state I hadn't previously witnessed in my cool-headed friend.

"There're soldiers shooting at students outside my dorm window!" he shouted.

"Soldiers shooting?" I asked, totally confused.

"Yeah, everybody's running!" There was some commotion in the background but I wasn't sure what was happening. "I'll call you back!" yelled Jim nervously.

"Wait! What's going on?" I asked. He had hung up. I called back three times but there was no answer.

On the news the following morning I saw what had shaken Jim so badly. Protesting the Vietnam War, several students at Kent State University had been gunned down (nine injured, four killed) by the Ohio State National Guard. It was a heartbreaking and senseless tragedy. Jim came home a day after the shootings. An eyewitness, he was almost as traumatized as when he initially phoned. In an attempt to cheer him up, I suggested, "Hey, let's go see Bev perform! She's been begging us to catch her act. I'll invite some of the other dancers also." I figured we could boost his morale and give Bev support at the same time.

"Outta sight!" shouted Bev when I called to let her know we'd be catching her set that night.

Bev was thrilled when we arrived at the West Side club, packed with about three hundred people. As she introduced our party of six to the owner as "My dear friends and fellow *Upbeat* Dancers," I couldn't help noticing that another dancer and I were the only black faces in the place. "Please take good care of them while I get ready for my set," said Bev to the owner. We were seated front and center and a cocktail waitress was instructed to "Give them whatever they want, on the house." No one seemed to mind that we were underage.

Bev looked impressive up on stage in front of a five-piece band. A royal blue micro-mini complimented her tanned skin and long straight yellow hair. Having never heard her sing, I didn't know quite what to expect. "I'd like to dedicate this first song to the best dancers in the world and my dearest friends, Jim and Arlee," she announced, smiling in our direction. I was flattered, then astonished, when out of the mouth of that seventeen-year-old white girl flowed a beautiful powerful voice, drenched in soul. Her gutsy rendition of Joe Cocker's, "I Get By With a Little Help From My Friends" sent chills down my spine. It earned her a standing ovation. Midway through her show, Bev made an announcement. "The *Upbeat* Dancers are in the house and I'd like them to join me on stage for my next number."

"Groovy!" shouted one patron above the enthusiastic applause.

As we proudly danced next to my friend singing her ass off on Otis Reddings "Can't Turn You Loose," I thought, "This girl's going to be a big star one day." (A month later she was given a singing spot on *Upbeat*.)

After the show, Jim, Bev, and I went to Bev's modest West Side home. Unlike Jim's, her parents always made me feel welcome. Mr. Jones, a jovial man of about forty, enjoyed telling corny, somewhat bawdy jokes. Extremely proud of his "princess," he pulled out the "Beverly Jones Scrapbook" for at least the millionth time. Mrs. Jones, an attractive petite woman in her thirties, liked reminiscing about "the good old days. I was quite a number in my day," she bragged,

Upbeat!

popping her fingers and prancing about. "Where do you think Bev gets it from?" After playing host for about half an hour, Mrs. Jones started yawning. "We'll leave you young folks alone," she said. "Arlee, remember, you're family. Don't be a stranger."

"I won't," I answered. Mr. and Mrs. Jones then headed upstairs to bed.

Jim, Bev, and I laughed and talked until dawn. Several months since the three of us spent time together, it had been a special night.

"I want to thank youse guys for getting me out of the house tonight," smiled Jim.

"*Youse* guys?" I laughed.

"Okay. *You* guys. It was great hanging out with two of my favorite people." Then Bev stood and raised an imaginary glass in a toast. She looked toward the ceiling and thought for a moment.

"Let's make a pact, guys. No matter what happens in our lives, no matter *what*, we will always be the Mod Squad, the best of friends." The three of us clasped hands, making the pact official.

Jim returned to school and all but left *Upbeat*. His busy schedule and a long commute only allowed for occasional appearances. Bev and I starting spending more time together, even became partners on the show for a short period. Things were going great for her. She had graduated from high school (Jim was her prom date). Not only did she dance on television, she was singing to packed houses every weekend. There was also a new boy in Bev's life and she was falling in love. On giving up on *Jim* romantically, she said, "I'll always love him as a friend and he's still my favorite dance partner. I'm happy the way it all turned out." She should have been. Her life looked like a straight clear road to success and happiness. At least that's the way it appeared at the time.

Home from school one weekend, I got a late-night call from Jim, sounding sad, like he had been crying. "What's wrong?" I asked, half asleep. At first he hesitated.

She Can Go Where Pretty Girls Go

Then he whispered, "Bev. Bev's gone."

"Gone where?" I asked still struggling to wake up.

"She's been in an accident, Arlee."

"An accident?" By then I was fully awake and starting to get scared. "Is she okay?"

"No."

"No? What do you mean, no?"

"Arlee, she's gone!" My heart sank.

"Jim, don't play!"

"I wish to God I was playing. A girlfriend was driving her home from the club she sang at when the accident happened. Her friend survived the crash. Bev wasn't so lucky."

"No, Jim! It can't be!" I groaned. "I have to call you back!" I slammed the phone down and sat completely quiet for a few minutes as Jim's words replayed in my mind. "She's gone, Arlee. She's gone." Then the screaming started. It was about a minute before I realized it was coming from me. My mother came running into my room. When I told her the horrible news, she broke down as well. My whole family did. Bev's mother was inconsolable when I called.

"You know she loved you, Arlee," she wept.

"Yes, Mrs. Jones, I know," I answered, trying hard not to cry. "I love her too." For weeks I was in a state of shock and disbelief, barely eating or sleeping. I don't remember much about the funeral. Only Bev lying peacefully in a bed of pink satin and my helping to carry a pink coffin down some church stairs. Bev's death had been the most painful thing I had experienced. It would take me years to get beyond it. The only thing that kept me grounded was *Upbeat* and the dancers.

By 1971 I had been dancing on *Upbeat* for three years. The show had been on the air for seven but there seemed to be some concern about its future. I had heard the show was having problems getting sponsors, something to do with cigarette ads. That year tobacco ads were banned on television and advertisers were unsure about their programming. I wasn't sure what that had to do with us, since I never remembered seeing any cigarette commercials during *Upbeat*'s broadcast. As the year moved on we did fewer tapings. The show eventually started showing reruns. Then came the day we all dreaded. The entire cast was called into the studio. Producer Herman Spero spoke: "*Upbeat* has been cancelled due to a lack of sponsors. Thank you for your contributions in making the show *so* popular for *so* long." Each dancer was then given a letter of thanks and recommendation and small tokens of appreciation: sterling money clips with *Upbeat* inscriptions for the guys and jewelry boxes for the girls. Everyone was crushed! Some even cried. The show had been the biggest part of our lives. Certain to miss the prestige and attention, mostly we would miss one another. With Bev gone and now the show, life felt empty and the previous three years seemed like a dream.

I'm not sure I could have gotten through everything if it wasn't for my final and favorite *Upbeat* partner, Jackie Carson. We became partners after Gail Philpott left the show two years earlier to attend college. Jackie helped me get through losing Bev. We helped each other get over the loss of the show. The only person, other than my sister Deb, whom I could confide in, Jackie seemed to have the answers to many of my questions. Brown-skinned and attractive with big starry eyes, a "big fly fro," and loads of panache, she was a hard-working and talented dancer as well, always coming up with new and creative ways of making us look even better. With her as my partner we won the Plain Dealer Dance Contest the previous year. Named the best in northeastern Ohio, we were presented with a trophy and five hundred dollars. Another memorable time was when we performed (outside) at "Fun Day On the Mall." As well as being cheered in a parade, we danced alongside BJ Thomas, The O Jays, and Edwin Starr, performing his smash hit "War." We also got a chance to meet Cleveland's impressive new mayor, Carl B. Stokes, a sponsor of the show—and the first black mayor of such a large American city.

Since there were no longer any shows to do, I spent most of my time at Jackie's East Cleveland home. Her mom Clarice Nicholson, stepdad Al, and five brothers accepted me as an honorary member of the family. I frequently went to Mrs. Nicholson for advice. Ever optimistic and one of the wisest people I knew, she could inject some good in even the most horrible situations. Supportive of Jackie's and my dancing as well, she had frequently attended our television tapings and live performances, critiquing every gesture. I called her my stage mom, but she was much more.

With Mrs. Nicholson's help, Jackie and I seriously contemplated our uncertain post-*Upbeat* futures. She decided on college, applied to, and was accepted at the University of Cincinnati. I decided to "find myself." One afternoon, as we were shopping and taking in the sights downtown, Jackie and I happened past the old Allen Movie Theatre. Tired and needing a place to relax for a couple of hours, we decided to go in. We had no idea what the movie was about. The marquee read *The Christine Jorgensen Story*.

Set in the midfifties and based on a true story, the low-budget film was about a man named George Jorgensen who had always felt he was really female. Stunned, I thought, "There's someone else in the world like me?" With great interest I watched as Jorgensen went for medical help. I was flabbergasted when a doctor told him his problem could be corrected surgically. Jorgensen traveled from the United States to Denmark to have the procedure done. "Something can actually be done about my problem?" I thought. I wept right there in the theatre! Having confided in Jackie the previous year, she and I looked at one another. We both knew what I had to do.

Mama Annie Bell in a dress (a rare occurrence) and Auntie Gertrude visiting a relative in Boston, Mass. (late 1940s).

In Carlisle, South Carolina: Granddaddy "Bo-cat" and Grandma Eula Bell with Willie Lewis, one of their thirteen children.

She Can Go Where Pretty Girls Go

At home in Longwood Garden Apartments in Cleveland, Ohio (1968). Standing, left to right: Me, mother Effie, her boyfriend Walter, sister Ernestine's baby Sonya, and sister Deb. Seated, left to right: Brother Lester and Uncle Mack. (Older sister Ernestine took the picture)

My father Arlee "Red Gip" Gibson in the late seventies.

Upbeat!

Cover of Plain Dealer TV Guide, July 31, 1970. That's me on the far left and atop the U. Sideburns courtesy of Maybelline eyebrow pencil.

She Can Go Where Pretty Girls Go

The "Mod Squad": Me at far left, Bev Jones front left, next to her, Jim Stallard. Remaining *Upbeat* dancers: Mary Lynn, Jackie Carson, Linda Mulcahy, Kim Havrilla, John Magill, Carolyn, Jean Hagedorn, Diane Rini, Arline Burks, Peggy Miller.

Maurice "Hank" Nystrom: *Upbeat* choreographer during show's heyday.

BLACK BUTTERFLY

*H*aving performed at cabarets and clubs from ages thirteen through sixteen, at seventeen I was no stranger to nightlife. The Flair Bar offered my first look into *gay* nightlife. The popular downtown spot played host to a colorful cast of characters during the late sixties and early seventies. I first went with a friend of the family, Mom's ex-boyfriend Westley's nephew Butch, openly gay and a regular. Never having been around a group of gay people, I felt somewhat apprehensive about going.

As we approached the bar apprehension quickly turned into fear. Right outside the entrance, a huge black man was pounding another man's head against the sidewalk pavement. A gathered crowd watched in horror but no one stepped forward to help. Suddenly, the giant let go of his victim and stared directly at me. I wanted desperately to turn and walk away, but gripping fear prevented any bodily movement. "Hey, Upbeat! You're my favorite dancer!" he yelled, a broad smile stretched across his dark round face. The poor guy he had been pulverizing welcomed the diversion and grasped the opportunity to run for his life. Totally forgetting about his victim, the three-hundred-pound-plus assailant began doing vigorous showgirl kicks,

Black Butterfly

humming *Upbeat*'s theme music—badly. It was hard to believe the effeminate can-can dancer before me was the same brute that savagely beat a man just minutes earlier. Finding it grimly humorous, I laughed—cautiously.

My new fan, introduced as "Big Mama," offered an explanation for the fracas. "I'm the bar's bouncer and a drunk got out of line." He escorted Butch and me inside and went out of his way to make us welcome. The small bar, predominantly white and male, was jam-packed and the music, good and loud. But it was weird seeing men dancing together. Every seat was taken so Big Mama asked two men seated at the bar to relinquish theirs. I was introduced to the Flair's owner, a friendly little old white man named Harry who stood guard behind the bar. He spoke through a surgically placed contraption in his throat. In a robotic voice he complimented my dancing on *Upbeat*, then said to the bartender, "All Upbeat's drinks are on the house!" I thanked him and tried not to look nauseated when he pulled out a handkerchief and blew his nose through his throat.

After two rum-and-cokes I was ready to brave the small crowded dance floor. When Johnnie Taylor's "Who's Making Love" played on the jukebox, I got up and did my thing. A pretty black lady seated nearby began staring. I thought she was admiring my moves, so I danced harder. Then suddenly, at the top of her high-pitched voice, she screeched, "You're late and you're tired, Miss Upbeat! *Late-and-tired*!

"Am I actually being heckled?" I thought. "And did she actually say *Miss* Upbeat?" The lady stood and brazenly stepped toward me. What she did next was completely unnerving. Over the loud music, she screamed *Upbeat*'s theme music uncomfortably close to my ear, then cackled defiantly. Fed up, I turned and said, "That'll be enough, Mister!" suspecting she was a drag queen because of her cockiness, mannerisms, and use of gay slang. She was outraged!

"Step outside, yellow bitch!" she demanded as she headed toward the front of the bar.

Butch rushed to my side with an emergency warning. "That is the notorious Tracy St. Clair and you do *not* want to fuck with her!" A small group scurried over to get a closer look at the fool who had dared to insult Tracy.

One man said, "Tracy's a working girl and armed robber!"

Another claimed, "Miss Thing has even murdered before!"

A third stranger slipped me a small knife, cautioning, "Tracy will surely have hers." I didn't really want to fight but backing out in front of everyone wasn't an option. It would mean open season on my butt if I ever returned to the bar.

As Tracy and I stormed toward the exit Big Mama intervened. Grabbing both of us by the arm as if we were misbehaved children, he swiftly led us downstairs into the bathroom. "Everybody out!" he yelled, causing a scramble for the bathroom's exit. A defiant muscle-bound drag queen in a too-tight silver lame mini didn't budge. Big Mama introduced her as Miss Denise. Reeking of cheap perfume, her makeup was kabuki-white, a contrast to her dark arms and legs. Her stiff platinum wig looked more like headgear than hair. As Big Mama chastised Tracy, the "fright" queen listened attentively. "Upbeat is good people and no one's going to fuck with her!" Big Mama warned.

"Ah, true!" croaked Miss Denise. Tracy looked as relieved as I did that no blood would be shed that night. She apologized, gave me a hug, and we marched arm in arm upstairs.

"I like the way you stood up to me," she said. "Have a drink on Mother."

I spent the rest of the evening hanging out with Tracy who I found to be riotously witty and a full-fledged drama queen. At one point she snatched off an "undetectable" shag wig to reveal her own hair, snatched in a chic chignon. Tracy had style. Her tall, slim frame was perfectly fitted in tan hip-huggers and a plunging V-necked blouse, which revealed a pair of real breasts. I tried my best not to stare but a man with breasts was shocking. Unable to contain my curiosity, I asked her to tell me about the "miracle." "Female hormones," she said. Weekly injections of estrogen gave her body a more feminine appearance: Breast and hips formed, the voice becomes higher, facial and body hair thinned. It was all so unbelievable! I wanted to know more, but Tracy quickly grew bored with my inquisition. To my complete surprise and utter delight she suddenly stood up, arms outstretched, and belted out Barbara Streisand's "People" as well as Streisand herself. The bar silenced for the spell binding performance. The undisputed diva of the Flair Bar was rewarded for her impromptu concert with a roaring ovation. My first night at the Flair was quite a learning experience and certainly one of the most *different* evenings I had ever spent.

I returned to the Flair nearly five months later. Big Mama, Tracy and I held a private reunion just outside with me crying laughing as they dished (talked about) everyone who walked by. "Alright, Miss Bernadette girl! You're locking!" (looking good) Tracy screamed sarcastically at a figure approaching from the distance.

"Pee girl!" (looking fabulous) added Big Mama, snickering. Marching towards us, forcefully switching her narrow hips from side to side, was a skinny drag queen in a horrendous red patent-leather vest and miniskirt ensemble. Matching knee-high boots, designed to fit snugly, hung droopily around her bony legs. She stopped directly in front of me and slowly looked me up and down, a big "Diana Ross" wig all but covering one of her overpainted eyes. Stretching her long neck to one side, she tapped twice on her chest.

"Alright, Miss Upbeat! I watched you a boogalooin' on TV ev'ry week!" she shouted. "You'd be a-sockin' it to em!" Then she broke out in a hyper spastic impression of me dancing. Big Mama and

She Can Go Where Pretty Girls Go

Tracy laughed and joined in on the jig. "Yo big lard ass as light as a feather," said Bernadette to Big Mama with a half-sincere grin.

At that moment a white blond man in glasses pulled up in a shiny white Cadillac convertible. It was Tracy's longtime boyfriend coming to fetch her. Dressed in a long fitted black dress and gold flat sandals, Tracy entered the luxurious automobile with the attitude of a socialite. Comfortably seated, she called out to Bernadette in a sweet singsong voice, "Sissies walk and take buses. A woman rides in luxury." With a loud half-circled snap of her finger she sped off.

"Aaaa dirty bitch," Bernadette snarled just before shifting her attention to a group of five men passing on their way to the bar. Like a cat stalking its prey, she zeroed in on one of them—dressed in both male and female attire. Apparently he had offended her during a previous encounter. Bernadette began poking Big Mama with her sharp elbows, puckering, exaggeratedly pointing at the man. Then at the top of her voice she screamed, "You there, looking like that there!" The poor fellow turned to face his tormentor but said nothing. "Looking as hard as times were in the thirties, you'll *never* be the woman I am. Cause you're late, late, *lateeee*!" Bernadette lambasted, her moderately feminine voice growing deeper with each "late." For added emphasis, she snapped her fingers hard and loud in the man's face, barely missing his nose. The poor guy just stood there dumbstruck as his friends looked on. Then Bernadette turned to Big Mama and grinned devilishly. "Should I give the dirty cockeyed bitch a severe knock across the snout?" she asked. Wisely advised to end the assault, Bernadette dismissed the terrified man with a word of caution. "The next time you git in my face, I'mmo do more then jus 'read.' We gonna lock asses!" The act of annihilating someone verbally was called "reading" in the gay world and Bernadette had raised it to an art form. She also had a reputation as a tough street fighter that few challenged.

I liked Bernadette. Though a little rough, there was a genuine womanly quality about her. Initially, I was embarrassed to be seen with her. The garish makeup and wardrobe along with her outlandish behavior was out of place in "normal" society. She wore a tough exterior, but just underneath was a positive, kind, and loving "woman" who always succeeded at lifting everyone's spirit with her sick brand of humor. Even though she had little, Bernadette would give her last to a friend in need. Gradually, those qualities won me over and I began to care little about what others thought.

When I first visited Bernadette I was shocked by the living conditions. She lived with her grandparents in the basement of a dilapidated four-story building on Carnegie Avenue. Half the basement housed the building's antique heating furnace and maintenance equipment. The other half had been transformed into a tiny two-and-a-half-room apartment that Bernadette and her grandparents called home. The front door led into a kitchenette. Faded curtains were used in place of doors throughout the rest of the apartment. I was invited to have a seat in the living room, which was dark and crammed with bulky old furniture. Bernadette graciously offered refreshments: Vienna sausages, saltines, and cherry Kool Aid. Then with a look of seriousness in her eyes she sat down next to me and began staring at my face. "What's wrong?" I asked uneasily.

"You know you're really a girl, Miss Two. Don't you think it's time you started *looking* like one?" Abruptly, before I could even respond, my hostess stood then left the room. She returned moments later carrying a pink vinyl makeup case. "You're in capable hands, Miss Thing," she assured me as she prepared for the challenge of transforming a seventeen-year-old boy into a beautiful woman. Apprehension, nervousness, excitement—that's what I felt, never having dressed as a girl before—unless you count the time I sneaked into my mother's tight black fringed dress.

She Can Go Where Pretty Girls Go

As Bernadette applied my makeup she began telling me about her life. "I'm twenty-two and my birth name is James Doss. I never knew my father, and my mother, who I call Miss L'il, is in the looney bin." Sharing some of her most painful childhood memories, she recalled being abandoned for days at a time and countless beatings. Bernadette received little schooling and could barely read or write. To support herself she resorted to prostitution and stealing at the young age of fourteen. As she continued layering on my makeup, Bernadette shared some details about her not-so-distant past. "I just got out the clink [prison] a couple a months ago, Miss Two. Me and two other queens tried to hijack a eighteen-wheeler, but we were snatched up by Alice [the police]. We were arrested, found batty as hell, and sentenced to Lima State Penitentiary." Bernadette served three years.

After an hour and a half of plucking, painting, and powdering, my makeup was finally done. Bernadette looked pleased. Then she plopped what looked like a buzzard's nest on my head and vigorously teased and brushed it. Satisfied with my hair, she took me to her closet, just two feet away, for wardrobe. She reached inside the cluttered dark hole and pulled out an outfit. "You the only person I'd let bump in my best l'il breakin'-it-up number," she said proudly. I almost choked! On the bent wire hanger hung the same horrible red patent-leather suit she had on when I first met her!

My transformation was complete. Bernadette sniffled, "Miss Two, you look so, so pretty, like fish [a real woman]: pure tuna."

"Really?" I asked doubtfully.

"No one would ever know."

Forbidden to see myself during the makeover, I was finally given the okay to look in a mirror. It was quite a challenge seeing past showgirl lashes glued to my top *and* bottom lids, but once I did focus, I cringed. The thick pancake foundation was at least three shades too dark and I had the same overteased hairstyle as Bernadette. Dressed in her ugly red patent leather suit, I *looked* like her! I absolutely hated my makeover but couldn't bring myself to tell Bernadette. I forced "Thank you, girl, you did a great job" from my mouth, but the drag queen hooker look was the complete opposite of the clean modern image *I* had in mind.

"What name are you gonna use?" Bernadette asked, still sniffling with pride.

"Connie," I answered quickly. I had waited a long time to use that name openly.

"Okay, Miss Connie *girl*, it's now time for your public debut."

"Ohhh no!" I said. "I am not going outside looking like this!"

"But Sister Belle, you look so pretty. And you gotta go out sometimes. Now's a good a time as any."

Strong as a team of oxen, Bernadette proceeded to pull me from her apartment onto the street. Begrudgingly, I walked with her about ten blocks to visit a girlfriend of hers, certain everyone we passed knew I wasn't a girl. To my surprise, we went about our business virtually unnoticed. A couple of men even flirted. "People must think we're just two crazy ladies with extremely bad taste," I thought. Although I appreciated all she had done, I was relieved when we got back to Bernadette's apartment, and it was a pleasure returning my look to its rightful owner. I was grateful as well to her grandmother who extended an open invitation to "dress" at their home, something I couldn't do at my own. I started going out as Connie once or twice a week.

I was caught totally off guard the first time Bernadette visited *me*, unannounced and uninvited. When I answered the door and saw her standing there in a ridiculous polka dot halter mini and idiotic grin, my jaw dropped. "How did she find out where I live?" I wondered. "Mom's going to *kill* me!" Before I could utter a word, Bernadette barged right in and made herself comfortable at the dining table.

She Can Go Where Pretty Girls Go

I almost passed out when Mom yelled from upstairs, "Who was at the door?"

"What am I going to say?" I thought. "That my new drag queen friend is visiting?"

"Who was at the door?" Mom yelled again—this time much louder. When I took too long answering, she came downstairs to see for herself. I panicked and ran out of the house, stood just outside the door, and waited for the fireworks. There was total silence. Unable to just abandon my guest (and just a little curious), I went back inside to face the consequences. Imagine the look on my face when I found Mom and Bernadette talking and laughing—like long-time best girlfriends.

"Miss Effie girl, I'm feeling a l'il lunchy. Got any vittles?" asked Bernadette.

Mom laughed as she put a Bobby "Blue" Bland album on the stereo. Recognizing one of the songs, Bernadette screamed, "Ahhhh, 'Further on up the Road,' Miss Effie! I say I feel right *garbage* cannish; throw me in the alley!"

"You a mess, girl," Mom laughed. "Junior, fix ya comp'ny somethin' to eat. There's some souse meat, goose liver, and pop in the 'frigerator."

"Yeah, girl, rustle up some grub while me and Miss Effie have a l'il chitchat," ordered my uninvited guest. Bernadette kept calling me *girl* and *Connie*. Mom didn't react, but I knew it disturbed her.

Bernadette became a frequent guest in our home. Mom and Deb adored her while Lester and Walter tolerated her. We *all* enjoyed her offbeat, biting humor. "Y'all the family I never had," said Bernadette.

As our friendship grew Bernadette and I began hanging out together, mostly at the Flair, which had a packed house seven nights a week. Business was so good the bar's owner decided to expand. Harry opened a larger spot on Fifty-seventh and Euclid and named it the Scope Club. The clientele was much like that at the Flair, predominately gay white males. Unless you counted the clientele, music from a jukebox was the Flair's only entertainment. Harry wanted to feature live entertainment at the new club, equipped with a half-circle stage and overhead theatrical lightning. His right-hand man Big Mama, put in charge of recruiting talent, offered me the position of go-go dancer. "What?" I said, half disgusted. Dancing on his toes and popping his fingers, Big Mama tried to make the job sound appealing.

"Girl, you'll be on stage dancin' in a cute little red fringed bikini; just *givin'* it to the fellas!"

"Now Big Mama. To suggest that a dancer of my caliber should stoop to performing half naked in a second-rate fag bar is an outrage, a downright insult!"

"The pay's a hundred fifty dollars for two nights a week, Miss Thing."

"What color did you say that bikini was?" Broke and without options, I silently rationalized, "At least I can work as Connie."

My debut as the Scope's go-go dancer was a complete disaster! Dancing half bare on a riser, with men yelling out whatever nasty thing entered their minds, made me feel dirty. After only two records, I ran to the dressing room and got dressed. Harry insisted I finish out the night but I flatly refused. As Arlee I had established an excellent reputation as a dancer and was unwilling to compromise it by becoming a cheap go-go dancer in my new life. My entire life as Arlee was gone, the *good* as well as the bad.

Although I refused the dancing job, I did accept Harry and Big Mama's offer to perform in a drag show. Bernadette, Big Mama, and I did a spoof on the Supremes' "Up the Ladder to the Roof" with three-hundred-and-something-pound Big Mama as lead Jeannie Terrell (Diana had just left the group). It was wild! Everyone

She Can Go Where Pretty Girls Go

loved the show and I made a hundred dollars, my primary reason for signing up for a second one.

The Scope Club was filled to capacity for the second drag show. I received an ovation for my lip-synched performance of Melba Moore's "I Got Love" from the Broadway musical, *Purlie*, but was ill prepared for the show's big finale. Big Mama, a white queen named Diane, and I performed "You Gotta Have a Gimmick" from the movie *Gypsy*. My character was Miss Electra, a burlesque stripper who naughtily incorporated electric lights into her act. Whenever she shimmied, strategically placed bulbs lit up. I had only rehearsed the number twice and had never practiced using the lights. My flesh-tone leotard was draped in thin strands of tiny clear Christmas tree bulbs. A stagehand was instructed to turn my lights on when cued.

I lip-synched, danced, and strutted across the stage like it was opening night on Broadway. As the time neared for my big special effects I raised both arms in preparation. As soon as I shimmied the stagehand lowered the house lights and pulled the switch, right on cue. My body felt as if it had just been struck with a thousand bolts of electricity! Shrieking and jerking each time the switch was pulled, it looked (and felt) like I was being electrocuted. The audience loved it! They laughed and applauded my every agonizing moment. The finale received a standing ovation and three curtain calls. Despite the special-effects mishap, it was fun doing the show. I survived being roasted alive and had earned some desperately needed cash.

Bernadette didn't perform that night but was at the club with her new boyfriend. She looked radiant. Within a period of three months she had metamorphosed from a dated drag queen into a modern stylish lady. She had also fallen in love with a handsome white man who adored her as well. They moved into a two-bedroom apartment on the West Side with plans to marry soon.

Black Butterfly

Rarely venturing east, Bernadette was in the process of totally changing her lifestyle, including an upcoming sex change operation.

"You locked!" complimented Bernadette, grinning and snapping her fingers in my face. "You looked like a fishy little Christmas tree." Then, along with her boyfriend, she burst out laughing. "Girl, we're ready to leave. It's two in the morning, and Mother needs her beauty rest. Would you like a ride home in the plush Caddy?" she offered, referring to her boyfriend's new Cadillac. With a bottle of champagne waiting backstage and still basking in adulation, I wasn't ready to leave just yet. Besides, the club's owner wanted to speak with me.

"Girl, you can go," I said.

"You sure, Miss Two?"

"Yeah, I'll be fine. You know I only lived a short bus ride away."

My meeting with Harry was brief. He asked if I'd be interested in performing at the club on a regular basis. I refused. Though I could definitely use the money, being a professional female impersonator wasn't something I aspired to. As closing time drew near I began to regret letting my ride go. The area was notorious at night. Cruising in the Caddy with Bernadette would have been *much* better than taking a bus late at night.

The corner bus stop at Fifty-fifth and Euclid was well lit, but deserted. Over twenty-five minutes passed and there wasn't a bus in sight. Getting nervous, I contemplated walking the twenty blocks, thinking, "Maybe I'll see a bus as I'm walking or even luck up on a taxi." Just as I sold myself on the advantages of walking, an old beat-up gray station wagon pulled alongside the curb and stopped directly in front of me. I tensed as I counted five black men in the car. The one in the front passenger seat yelled out, "You wanna ride?"

"No thanks," I answered, easing away from the bus stop, preparing to run. Suddenly, with split-second timing the man jumped

She Can Go Where Pretty Girls Go

out the car, grabbed me, and stuck a gun in my side. He wrestled me into the car's front middle seat.

"I'll blow yo goddamn head off if you scream!" he threatened through clenched teeth. The gap-toothed driver grinned sinisterly before speeding away, running the intersection's red light. As I sat there petrified, trying to gather my thoughts, the men joked about sex acts they were planning to perform on me. The filthy language combined with overpowering breath and body odor made my stomach turn. And just as I thought, "Could things get any worse?" I glanced in the rearview mirror and noticed *another* carload tailing us. My heart raced, but I had to keep cool if I was going to survive. There was little doubt they were planning to rape me. "If they remove my clothing and find out I'm not a real girl, they're going to *kill* me," I thought. I had to find a way out. Pretending to go along with my abductors, I assured them there was no need for violence. My stomach knotted as I purred in my sexiest voice, "All of you are kinna cute. Park the car now and let's get started." I didn't want to be taken too far into unfamiliar territory. They let down their guard some and even laughed and joked with me. Nervously laughing along I wondered, "How many women have fallen prey to this scum?"

My kidnappers pulled into an unlit vacant lot as I counted two small apartment buildings and one house on the short block. The second carload followed, parking about ten feet away. Struggling to remain calm I told the gunman seated next to me, on the passenger side, "I want you first." The vile-smelling trio in the backseat got out and stood on the driver's side while the driver remained in the car. It was time to make my move. I gave the gunman a tensed smile, then asked him to "Get out and get the backseat ready." He got out but only for a second.

"I can get everything ready from inside," he said kneeling in his seat, facing toward the back.

Noticing he had left the door opened, I thought, "It's now or never." As fast and as hard as I could I pushed him out of the car, leaped out and over him, then ran for my life. "Fire!" I screamed as I ran for an apartment building about fifty feet away. Frantic, I rang every single bell but no one answered. "I've got to get out of here!" I thought." When I ran from the building, seven extremely angry men were waiting.

"Fuckin' bitch!" one yelled.

"Bust a cap in her ass!" yelled another. Fearing being shot, I ran as fast as I could, zigzagging to make myself a more difficult target. With my pursuers close behind, I concentrated on a lit window in the house a few yards away.

"Please let me in, they're going to kill me!" I screamed, banging on the front door. Suddenly the door flung open and a large hand reached out and snatched me in. A man of around fifty quickly turned off the lights as his wife tried calming me down. "You poor little thing," she said. "We saw the whole thing and already called the police." I thanked them, breathless and still terrified, and asked to use the phone. Unbelievably, when I peeped through the curtain, my kidnappers were still outside. And they didn't leave—until two carloads of my friends arrived. The couple who saved my life advised me to wait for the police. I just wanted to go home and forget the entire frightening experience.

I told Mom about the incident, adding, "If you would just let me dress the way I want at home, I wouldn't have to hang in the streets so much." It was extremely inconvenient. Since Bernadette no longer lived at her grandparents', I didn't feel comfortable getting dressed there. A girlfriend who worked as a desk clerk at the Park Lane Motel sometimes let me use one of the vacant rooms there. After awhile I got tired of lugging clothes around and began using our complex's laundry room, conveniently located just steps from our front door.

Things gradually got better at home. Eventually I was allowed to wear foundation and mascara, but no blush, eye shadow, or lipstick. Certain girl tops and pants were okay, dresses weren't. Mercifully, Mom and Walter stopped calling me Junior but still refused to call me Connie. They had their *own* name for me—Suzy Cat—later shortened to Suzy. But a name compromise wasn't enough: I wanted to be accepted for who I was. The time had come for me to assert myself.

My best friend Jackie Carson had just come home, on break from classes at the University of Cincinnati. She phoned, asking if I wanted to go dancing at the "Afro Set" that evening. "As long as I can borrow an outfit from your fly wardrobe," I answered.

"I have just the thing for you," said Jackie, "a little something I picked up in Cincinnati. We're going to have so much fun! I'm excited, aren't you?"

"Yeah, The music at the Afro Set is fly and the guys, *butter*fly!" We both screamed.

Overhearing the conversation, my sister Deb shouted, "I wanna go!"

"Great!" I said. "It'll be girl's night out!"

"I'm going to come by your place early and get dressed there," said Jackie.

College life agreed with Jackie. She looked sophisticated in a camel pantsuit and new "Joan of Arc" hairstyle. I rushed her past my mother, uncle, and two of their friends seated at the dining table, upstairs to my bedroom. Anxiously waiting was Deb, excited about our night out. After catching us up on her life in Cincinnati and her new pretty-boy drug dealer boyfriend with money to burn, Jackie decided we should start getting dressed. "You and Deb can get ready now," I said. "I'm not allowed to dress at home. I can put my makeup on here but I have to get dressed in the laundry room."

"The laundry room?" Jackie shuddered. "That's ridiculous! You've got to stand up for yourself! The three of us are getting dressed right here and marching down those stairs and straight out the door!" Deb and I just stood there, speechless.

Finally Deb said, "Sure, Connie, why not?" A few reasons came to mind, my mother, uncle, and their friends. I would have to walk right past them to get to the front door.

I loved the black fitted jumpsuit Jackie brought for me, and the burnt-orange, crushed velvet mini she was wearing. Deb wore her new tan knit hot-pants set. After I put on my crowning glory, brushed and blended it, we were ready to leave. It took all the courage I could muster up to walk down those stairs. First, I took a deep breath. Then, with Jackie leading I followed closely behind, trailed by my scared sister. When we walked past Mom and her friends, they suddenly stopped talking. I didn't *dare* look. My eyes remained fixed on the front door. Once outside, I was able to breathe again. "I'll deal with the consequences later," I thought. My best friend was home from school and it was time to party.

Mom was furious the following day. "Deb, you only fifteen and have the nerve to stay out 'til four in the mornin'?" She was angrier with me. "I don't want you dressin' like that in this house, embarrassin' me in front of my friends and neighbors!" Hurt, but even more confused, I felt she should be more concerned about how I viewed her friends, which included a prostitute, gamblers, and drunks. It had come time for me to move.

I needed to get my own place but had no idea how I was going to come up with the money. I lacked the confidence to seek employment as Connie. Being a high school dropout didn't help matters. After careful consideration, I decided to apply for emergency public assistance. Having been on a program called ADC (Aid to Dependent Children) under my mother's name, at

She Can Go Where Pretty Girls Go

eighteen I was eligible to apply for assistance on my own, as an adult. It only allowed for three months of support, which was fine with me. I had felt ashamed being a welfare child and vowed I wouldn't become a welfare adult. However, needing an apartment immediately, there was little time for false pride.

At the Flair Bar one night, I met a drag queen named Jackie Las Vegas—twenty-five, weathered, but somewhat real-looking—who told me about an affordable vacant apartment near the street she lived on. "Miss Thing, it's on Eighty-sixth in Euclid and it don't look like it cost much." I took a bus the following day to check out the place. A band of drag-queen prostitutes were gathered on the corner—not a good sign. Remaining optimistic, I walked down the block until I came to the address Jackie Las Vegas had given me. The rundown two-story building looked abandoned. As I peeped through a small window at the top of the locked front door, I rang the only working bell but there was no answer. I persisted until finally, a man appeared at the top of the stairs. About twenty, dark, well dressed, and nice-looking, he cautiously walked down the stairs, holding a gun down by his side.

"What you want?" he asked.

"Any apartments available?" I answered, nervously loud. He opened the door.

"Follow me!" he said. Desperate for a place of my own, I obliged.

We entered an apartment near the top of the stairs. Four young men sat in the living room watching TV. I couldn't tell how many more were in an adjoining room because the door was quickly shut. Two guns lay in clear view on the coffee table. Nervously, I introduced myself and asked, "Do you have any vacancies?"

"Right on!" said one fellow as he reached into his pocket and handed me two keys on a ring, no questions asked. The man who let me into the building volunteered to show the place, located just across the hall.

Black Butterfly

Cozy, clean, and completely furnished; the apartment had a small living room, even smaller bedroom, and large sunny kitchen. "How much?" I asked my prospective landlord, introduced as Lewis. He grinned.

"Free, if you be my lady."

"Be your what? I'm looking for an apartment, not a boyfriend."

"Come on now, Red. Don't be like that."

"Be like what? I'm looking for a place to stay and you're standing there talking nonsense."

"Tell you what," he said. "Since you so cute, you can have the place for free—no strings attached. Just be real careful who you let in the building." Desperate, I accepted without asking a single question. The rent was certainly affordable.

I moved in immediately, with no source of income—but no bills either, not even for utilities. Having never lived alone, I missed my family. Being without a phone made it even worse. I was the only tenant in the building besides the guys next door, who checked in on me periodically. But unlike me, my neighbors had a steady stream of visitors, especially during the night. I found it strange that they always answered the door armed. "They sure are a paranoid bunch," I thought.

My neighbor Lewis visited daily, always flashing a wad of money. "All this could be yours if you was my lady," he grinned. I wasn't interested. He acted strangely at times, nodding and talking incoherently. I thought he was drinking too much. I *did* accept pocket change occasionally and Lewis made sure my refrigerator stayed full. He was my only company for the first couple of weeks. But even though I was lonely and broke, for the first time in my life I was being myself. I had Jackie Las Vegas to thank for that.

On my way home one afternoon I ran into Jackie Las Vegas. "Did you get the apartment I told you about, Miss Thing?" she asked.

"Yes, and thanks. You have to drop by sometime." She came by that very night with another drag queen, introduced as Shirdeen (wearing way-too-light pancake makeup and red lipstick that extended upward past the corners of her lips). She was noticeably upset after being greeted at the main entrance by Lewis holding a sawed-off shotgun.

"Miss Thing!" she shrieked. "Don't you know you're living in a drug house?"

"Drug house? What do you mean?" I asked.

"Herion! Smack! Shit! The drug house, girl! Don't tell me you livin' up in here and don't even *know*?" It was all beginning to make sense: the apartment full of guys, the guns, people going in and out at all hours of the night. Lewis always carried plenty of cash but didn't have a job.

After my guests left I went next door to confront my neighbors about Shirdeen's accusation. They laughed at me. Extremely upset, I stormed out and went back into my apartment with Lewis following, still laughing. "I thought you knew," he said. "I sell shit and I use it too. I'm gonna tell you something else. I seen you even before you moved in the building. Lotsa times! At the Flair Bar. I had a thang for you the first time I laid eyes on yo cute red ass."

"Lewis, could you please leave?" was the only thing I could think of to say. I wasn't happy about living in a drug house but I didn't move out either. There was no place else to go.

After discouraging Lewis's visits, it became unbearable sitting in my apartment alone most of the time. On weekends, I started going to the Red Carpet Lounge, nineteen blocks away, on 105th and Euclid. If I had money I took the bus, if not I walked. The club, which offered all-night dancing, was the same place Diane, Butch, and I did countless cabaret shows just three years earlier. While walking home from there one morning, around six, I heard male voices yelling from behind. "Hey, slim? Red?" I walked faster but so did they. "Hey, slow up! Why you wanna be like that?" I was preparing to run when suddenly, out of nowhere appeared a giant white dog, exposing a terrifying set of long sharp teeth. I slowed my pace, not wanting to antagonize the beast. He started walking alongside me. "I'm in real trouble," I thought. "A couple of idiots are following me and a mutant killer dog is right beside me." Never having seen one quite so large, frankly, I was more afraid of the dog. Then miraculously, the dog suddenly turned around and began growling and barking at my harassers. When he started toward them, they fled. Still scared but mostly grateful, I gave my oversized hero a cautious pat on the head and headed home. He followed. I named my new roommate Guardian because he wouldn't allow anyone to approach me unless given the okay. He hated Lewis and barked every time he passed my door. Guardian's formidable size scared everyone. With him, I felt safer and a lot less lonely.

Another reason I was no longer lonely was Jackie Las Vegas, who began visiting regularly. She came one day with a fourteen-year-old drag queen in tow named Dionne. "She a orphan," said Jackie Las Vegas. "Her only living relative is her grandmama who won't put up with her grandson dressing in girl's clothes. Miss Thing living on the streets. And you know I got a house full and can't take in *one* more."

Drag queens usually stuck together and helped one another. Discarded by families, most were unwanted embarrassments with no place to go except on the streets. The older more established "girls" helped the younger ones by providing food, shelter, and guidance. These households were usually quite large and served as families. Survival was extremely difficult. Many were poorly educated and too masculine in appearance to "pass," eliminating most employment possibilities. A large number turned to prostitution or "boosting" (stealing), consequently spending time in and out of jail. Being a drag queen was a harsh and unforgiving life.

"Can Dionne stay with you, Miss Connie?" asked Jackie Las Vegas.

"Girl, I-am-so-broke, but you know I can't just let a child live in the streets," I answered. Guardian seemed to like her so we added one more to the family. It was a struggle but I did my best to support a fourteen-year-old, a dog the size of a pony, and myself. My mother and aunt were a big financial help. I ran errands for Mom and continued to do Auntie's hair and clothes shopping.

After a month, Dionne moved out of my place and in with a young queen she had recently met. I saw her a couple of weeks later, on the corner with two other queens, flagging down cars. Saddened, I wondered how long *I* could survive with no real means of support.

Winter was fast approaching and I was without a suitable coat. All I had was a smelly old fake-leopard jacket Jackie Las Vegas had given me. Her friend Shirdeen and another queen named Tanjy dropped by for a visit one evening wearing stunning full-length red fox coats. "Where did you get them?" I asked, stroking the soft fur and daydreaming for a moment about how fabulous I would look in one.

"We boosted them," said Shirdeen.

"You mean you *stole* them?"

"Yeah, Miss Thing, it was easy. You should come along on our next job. All you have to do is pick out a coat and we'll get it for you." She looked out the corner of her eye at *my* coat, balled up next to her on the sofa. "You can no longer be seen in that rag you refer to as your coat. I just won't have it!" The fast-talker was convincing. Somewhat embarrassed, I told her, "I'll think about it."

Shirdeen and Tanjy returned to my apartment early the following morning. They were going "shopping" and invited me along. "You won't have to do anything Miss Connie," Shirdeen assured me, "just kinda tag along to see how easy it is." I must have been out of my mind that day. I went.

The career shoplifters chose The May Company as their target. When we arrived at the downtown store we headed directly upstairs to the fur department. The coats were intoxicatingly beautiful. Shirdeen and Tanjy checked and rechecked to make sure they weren't being watched. They removed two silver fox coats from their hangers, replaced them with the cloth ones they wore into the store, then put on the furs. "Do what we just did," they instructed me. Without thinking, I snatched a gorgeous full-length red fox off a hanger, replaced it with my old rag, and put on the new coat. The three of us walked as fast and as inconspicuously as we could down the escalator and out of the store. Once outside, we ran. I was about a block away when an elderly woman walked directly in front of me. Unwilling to just run over her, I stopped to go around. That split second would cost. Suddenly two large black security guards grabbed me from behind. I put up a struggle but was no match. They led me back into the store and detained me in a small room until the Cleveland police arrived.

I was cuffed and taken to a waiting squad car. It was humiliating being led out of the store as shoppers gaped and pointed. During our drive to the police station I asked the two officers, "What's going to happen to me?"

One answered, "You're going straight to jail and will probably be charged with grand larceny because the coat's very expensive." When I told the story of how I landed in the mess they seemed sympathetic.

"Choose your friends more carefully in the future," the other policeman advised. Boy, was he right. Shirdeen and Tanjy got

She Can Go Where Pretty Girls Go

away scott-free and there *I* was, sitting in the back of a police cruiser on my way to jail.

City Jail was noisy, overly active, and frightening. I was asked a million personal questions, fingerprinted, and photographed for a mug shot. A female officer led me into a room to strip-search me. Feeling uneasy, I informed her, "I'm not a real girl."

"You mean you're a lesbian?" she asked. "You have to undress anyway." After I explained more graphically, she sent for two male cops, one of whom was assigned to my search. Every cavity of my naked body was thoroughly checked during the dehumanizing experience.

I was allowed just one phone call before being locked up. After yelling and cursing, Mom said, "I'll see what Walter and me can do. I love you."

"I'm so sorry, Mom," I said. Tears came to my eyes as I hung up, but jail was no place to be seen crying.

I was led upstairs to where the male inmates were housed. "You'll be here for a few days and then transferred to County Jail to await a trail date," said one policeman. I remained silent. We walked down a long wide corridor lined with cells filled with inmates—mostly black. They made a big commotion, whistling and hollering "Put her in here!" as we passed.

"It must be a nightmare," I thought. "This couldn't really be happening." I was then placed in a large cellblock in the middle of the huge corridor. The policemen removed my handcuffs, then they left. The crash of that big iron door shutting behind them echoed throughout the corridor.

The large cellblock was where all the inmates congregated. Within the cellblock were several small cells. The place smelled of unwashed bodies and cigarette smoke. Unsure of what to do next, I stood near the front. A rough looking bunch seemed to be salivating in my direction. "This is certainly not the place for a cute 118-pound eighteen-year-old girl," I thought. When I noticed four men walking toward me, I put on a tough façade, hoping to deter trouble.

"What you in for?" one asked.

"Robbery!" I answered with the toughest look and stance I could muster.

"You cute," commented the largest man in the group. Then he volunteered his services as my "protector." "Step off!" he warned the others. That was fine with me. It would be much easier to defend myself against one man than the entire lot. My self appointed protector offered me a cigarette, which I refused, then proceeded to tell me "how things work around here. Everybody gits locked up inside the small cells at night: two men to a cell. Yo pretty ass gotta be real careful in here. Some of these niggas might try and fuck you! Cell with me so I can protect you." As he rambled on I wondered how I was going to survive in that awful place until my transfer to County Jail. I overheard a couple guys talking about the better conditions there.

A few hours after being served our dinner rations of one dry sandwich and a small carton of juiceless juice, it was lock-up time. "Two men to a cell!" one of two guards yelled out. My protector led me forcefully by the arm to a cell near the back of the block.

He clenched his huge fist near my face and threatened, "I'mmo fuck you up if you don't cell wit me!" When the guard came to lock us in, the protector shot me a threatening look.

"Guard!" I yelled out. "This man is trying to have sex with me!" The would-be rapist looked shocked at my betrayal. He denied everything. After verbally reprimanding the man, the guard placed me in a private cell; complete with a wooden slate of a bed and filthy exposed toilet. "At least I'm safe for the night," I thought.

I slept very little my first night behind bars. As inmates yelled, a million thoughts raced through my head. "What's going to become of me? What's my family doing at this very moment? Is my dog being cared for? Am I going to have to constantly deal with men trying to rape me?"

The following morning I was awakened by one of the guards, handing out breakfast—another cold sandwich and warm imitation juice. It had not been just a horrible nightmare. I was *really* locked up and in *big* trouble. I ate inside my cell, trying to figure out how to survive a second day. Knowing I wouldn't be able to make it on my own, I had checked out inmates the previous day to see who I should befriend. I noticed four men talking amongst themselves who seemed different from the others—older, safer. They conversed mostly about current events and their families. As soon as I finished eating I left my cell and went directly to where the "family men" had gathered.

Tactfully, I eased my way into their conversation about American politics as it applied to the black man, then inquired about each man's family, worth about two hours of dialogue. One man commented, "You're a bright girl. Why were you hangin' 'round that clown yesterday? You gotta be real careful 'bout the company you keep during your incarceration. There some crazzzy mothafuckas up in here!" The men looked out for me during my stay at City Jail. I continued to have my own private cell and thankfully remained chaste.

After five funky days without a shower, toothbrush, or change of clothing, I was transferred to County. Though I looked forward to getting cleaned up and eating warm food, I was scared as hell. I had no idea what County Jail would be like. After being processed, I was given a clean pair of regulation overalls and taken upstairs. Once again I had to walk down a huge corridor past countless cellblocks of whistling inmates—once again disproportionately black. But instead of putting me in one of the cells, my two armed escorts walked me to an area on the other side. When we stopped in front of a large steel door, one guard unlocked and opened it. I was pleasantly surprised. Instead of being caged in a cold filthy cell I was to be housed in what looked like a dormitory. There were ten male inmates in the large, spotless main room with ten properly made-up beds lined against two walls. A round dining table stood in the center. I was taken to a smaller more private room off from the main area and assigned a small comfortable looking bed. It was difficult at first to clearly see who my three roommates were in the dimly lit room.

Barbara was first to introduce herself. With brown chiseled features and long coarse black hair she looked like an attractive thirty-five-year old woman, but her masculine voice gave her away. Barbara was in County on a prostitution charge, but a year earlier had been paroled from prison where she served time for manslaughter. "I killed my ol' man for cheatin' on me," she said with little emotion. Initially charged with murder, Barbara hired a good lawyer who had the charges reduced to manslaughter.

"How much time did you get?" I asked wide-eyed.

"Seven years," she answered.

"Seven years?" I whispered. I thought it shocking that a person could murder someone and only get seven years!

Barbara introduced me to the rest of the gang. A pretty white longhaired blonde of about twenty-five posed on the bed as if being photographed for a fashion layout. She appeared soft and feminine in the dim light but her deep voice revealed she was also a drag queen. "I'm in on a lot of prostitution charges," Linda announced, "and I'm losing a lot of money cooped up in this bitch!" The last of my roommates was a handsome nineteen-year-old white boy named Danny, in for attempted murder. He attached himself to me immediately.

"Anything you need, just let me know," he offered, half-swooning. What I needed was a hot shower, some warm food, and a good night's sleep.

I hated being locked up, but if I had to be I was in the best possible place. Barbara became like a big sister. I demanded private bathroom time and always had one of my roommates guard the door whenever I showered. A man from the main room threatened me when he wasn't allowed to enter. Barbara heard and came to my defense. "Anybody wanna fuck with Miss Connie gotta go through me!" she said. The threat was taken seriously. Barbara had already beaten up someone from the main room for "disrespecting" her and everyone knew she was a convicted killer. Any inmate from the main room who wanted to enter our room had to have her permission.

Our semiprivate quarters was referred to as the "girl's dorm." Danny was the only "guy" permitted to bunk in the room, put there for protection from the general population. He became obsessed with me, not allowing me to lift a finger to do anything. Danny did my chores, bought my commissary, and gave me money.

The "trustees" spoiled me as well. Inmates given special privileges earned through some sort of honor system, they were trusted by the guards to go from cell to cell, dispensing linen, meals, commissary, and other permitted necessities. There was a small window above my bed facing the main corridor. Every morning my two favorite trustees tapped on it to see if I needed anything. One was a barber on the outside. He made sure my big curly afro stayed groomed. Another cut the sleeves off my jail coveralls and altered the waist for a more feminine fit. I was even let out of the dorm, but only for a few minutes at a time. Inmates at the other end of the corridor made such a commotion I was afraid they'd cause my privilege to be revoked.

Black Butterfly

I received many love notes, via the trustees, from the locked-down brothers across the corridor. They nicknamed me "Pretty Connie" and my roommates jokingly referred to me as the jailhouse pin-up girl. I had no real romantic interest in anyone, but one brother did get my attention. He had seen me in the corridor and began writing intelligent, sweet notes. Always signed "Love, Darryl," I looked forward to the notes even though I had never seen the author.

One afternoon there was a knock on the window above my bed. I answered; thinking it was one of the trustees. Instead a gorgeous man in his early-twenties with copper skin, short black curls, green eyes, and a big beautiful smile stood outside the window. I blushed when he said his name was Darryl. "You fine," he said, his eyes capturing the light like perfectly cut emeralds. "Can I hold you if I get in your room?" Unable to speak, I just stood there, half grinning, looking stupid. Then he gently pressed his full moist lips against the window and said, "I'll see you soon."

Darryl surprised me two days later by walking straight into my room. "Gimme a hug!" he demanded. Before I could say a word, he grabbed me then kissed me. Barbara and Linda swooned. Danny was seething. My suitor and I talked for about five minutes before a trustee ordered him to leave.

"He must've paid lovely coins to get into the girl's dorm," teased Barbara.

"*Major* ducats!" laughed Linda.

Darryl continued to write and visited occasionally during my stay at County. He wanted to see me on the "outside" upon his release in a few months, but I had no interest in having a relationship with anyone I met in jail. I was merely trying to have the best time possible under extremely ugly circumstances. My future looked bleak. I was in jail on a grand larceny charge and had no

She Can Go Where Pretty Girls Go

idea how much time I was looking at. All I could do was wait and kill time.

Barbara, Danny, and Linda passed the time playing cards. There was a game practically every night in the main room. One evening, my roommates tried talking me into a game of "tonk," which they were playing in *our* room. I hated card games, reminders of the noisy all-night card parties my mother hosted. But with nothing better to do, I decided to just go ahead and play. A man from the main room, the very one who had angrily protested my private showers, asked if *he* could play. With some reservation, we let him in. "Fifty cents a game! Everybody up!" said Barbara. Danny put me up and gave me three dollars and some change. "You deal, Miss Connie!" said Barbara. Tonk was the game of choice at my house—and I had learned it well. Winning practically every hand, I arranged all my money in a neat pile. "Game over for me," said Barbara placing her cards face down.

"I'm out too," said Linda.

"Yeah, me too," said Danny. In a desperate move to win his money back, the man from the main room reached into his pockets and pulled out two cherished old silver dollars. He slammed one down on the table.

"A dollar a hand!" he commanded! "One on one!"

Danny lit my king-sized Kool and I dealt the first hand. In tonk, the lowest hand won and mine was extremely low. I showed it, grinned, then retrieved the pot. When I won the second hand and the man's last silver dollar, I gloated, "Next!"

"You cheated! I want all my money back!" said the man.

"I won fair and square," I answered, calmly inspecting my winnings.

Suddenly, he exploded, "Bitch, I will kick yo yellow ass! Tryin' to put *me* in a trick bag!" Then he lunged at me. Danny quickly intercepted. He grabbed the man, then hauled off and punched

90

Black Butterfly

him square in the face. The man hit the floor—hard. Showing no mercy, Danny began kicking him.

"Please Danny, stop!" I yelled, afraid he might seriously injure or even kill the guy. I appealed to Barbara. "Please make him stop!" She totally ignored me.

"Kick that ass!" Barbara shouted. "He ain't nothing but a shit-starter *no* damn way!" I finally convinced Danny to stop beating the man, whose face by that time had become a bloody mess. Luckily he wasn't seriously injured.

The following morning one of the trustees told my roommates and me, "I heard what happened last night. That fucka deserved a ass beatin'. Do you know he tried to put a contract out on Pretty Connie?"

"A contract?" I chuckled.

"I'm dead serious!" he said.

"For real?"

"Straight up!"

"But why would anyone want me dead?"

"That crazy fool jealous cause Danny like you." Danny admitted the man made prior passes at him, but stopped after he threatened him.

"I heard the crazy ass bitch been in the nuthouse before," said Barbara, getting angrier at each revelation. The trustee said the man offered another inmate money to kill me. Thank God the inmate reported the incident to a guard. I was also grateful to the trustees, who had knowledge of almost everything that happened within the inmate population. They also told us that Danny's beating victim reported my roommates and me to the guards. We were forewarned to expect a visit that day.

Two guards showed up as expected to question us about the previous night. Our accuser reported that we had stolen his money and beaten him up. We admitted to gambling, but denied the theft accusation. "What about the beating?" asked one of the guards.

"The sore loser attacked me and Danny was merely defending me." I answered.

"Disciplinary action will still have to be taken," said the guard. "Consider yourselves lucky you're not getting additional jail time."

The guards led my three roommates and me out of the dorm and into the main corridor. We walked until we came to a large steel door. "You're going to be held in solitary confinement until further notice," one of the guards informed us. Our diets were to consist of only bread and water during the duration of our confinement. I was relieved when Barbara, Linda, and I were put in the same cell. Danny was caged farther down the corridor.

"Could things get any worse?" I thought. Not only was I in jail, I was in what the inmates commonly referred to as "the hole."

When the door slammed and locked behind us, the approximately ten-by-ten-foot room went dark. A small barred opening near the top of the door let in a sliver of light. We barely had room to move around, and sleep came hard with just a thin blanket between the concrete floor and us. At least we ate okay. Thanks to the trustees, who sneaked us food once a day.

After only two days in the hole I was ready to scream! We weren't allowed to wash and there was very little ventilation. In an attempt to keep our spirits up we sang Motown tunes—badly—enduring heckling by both guards and inmates. Ever loyal, the trustees joined in on our sing-a-longs. Danny sang from his cell down the corridor.

My partners in crime and I were overjoyed upon our release from solitary confinement. Having endured the hellhole for five eternal days and nights, we raced for the shower. By the time we returned to our room, Barbara was seething. "I want the squealing bitch that landed us in the hole!" she yelled. But he was nowhere to be found. According to the trustee, he had been moved to another facility and brought up on charges for conspiring to murder. Danny wasn't taking any chances. He began sleeping on the floor at the foot of my bed. Barbara and Linda kept an eye out for me as well. The three of us had become even closer during our stay in the hole—almost like family.

I missed my real family. I had spoken to my mother twice since my lock-up but had yet to see her. She and her boyfriend were busy trying to get a lawyer for my impending trial. I was ecstatic when a trustee told me, "I saw your name on the visitor's list."

A guard led me into the crowded visiting room. I spotted Mom and Deb right away, seated at a table, looking around. "Pretty Connie!" a few inmates called out as I made my way to my family. My mother and sister never looked more beautiful. My eyes watered, I hugged them tightly.

"Shoot, here we are, all worried, thinking you're gonna be looking all bad, and here you are, Miss Popularity," Deb laughed. Mom was more serious.

"Walter got a lawyer who said he could prob'bly git the grand larc'ny charge reduced to a misdemeanor," she said. A misdemeanor charge would carry a lighter sentence or even probation—no jail time. It was my first ray of hope since being arrested. Before Mom left she vowed, "This is the last time I bail you outta dumb shit!" I started to miss my family even before I returned to the dorm. I missed my freedom even more.

Nearly two months after my arrest the big day finally arrived, my day in court. Barbara instructed me on how to behave in front of the judge. Linda and Danny also offered pointers. It was time to say our good-byes. There was a good chance I wouldn't be returning. I hugged Barbara first. She had been a loyal friend who always had my back. Tearfully, she said, "You're pretty and smart and can do a helluva lot better with your life. Please don't wind up like me, Miss Thing." Linda, due to be released soon, told me what street corner she could be found on. Danny had been sulking all morning. I gave him a hug and peck on the cheek.

"Now promise me you'll keep in touch," he said as he handed me his parent's phone number. I also got a chance to say goodbye to my jailhouse crush Darryl. He gave me his family's number as well. I would never forget the kindness shown me during my incarceration, but I was ready to leave and never wanted to see anyone I spent jail time with on the outside.

My lawyer negotiated with the judge and had the charges reduced. I almost shouted when he sentenced me to "a year probation, no jail time." I vowed never do anything that might land me back behind bars and to be more careful selecting my friends. Freedom was sweet. Once again, life held endless possibilities.

MY JOURNEY TO ME

I moved back home and my family finally accepted me as Connie. Mom and I were enjoying an especially good relationship, even though she was recovering from a bout with depression. A year earlier she was shot in the stomach while standing in her doorway by a woman positioned across the street. Strong as any man, my wounded mother ran after the woman. She got as far as the street before falling down unconscious. It was like a horrifying nightmare, seeing my mother sprawled in the street, her eyes locked in a hollow stare. The woman who shot her was someone her live-in boyfriend Walter had been fooling around with. Mom was hospitalized for over a month but recovered and, against family wishes, reconciled with Walter. Miraculously, she discovered she was pregnant only three months after being released from the hospital. The following year she gave birth to a nine-pound, ten-and-a-half-ounce baby boy named Mario. Mom and Walter seemed happy for a couple of years. Then Walter's eyes began to wander and the rest of him soon followed. He moved out and married a third woman he had been seeing. Walter continued to spend time with his son and supported him financially. Mom saw to that.

She Can Go Where Pretty Girls Go

One by one, everyone started leaving. My oldest sister Ernestine, raised down South by our grandmother, had moved up to live with us when she turned eighteen. Unmarried with a one-year-old daughter named Sonya, she enrolled at Cuyahoga Community College and worked part-time. After graduating, she landed a secretarial job with Sohio Oil, married a mailman, and purchased a two-story brick house. My brother was next to leave. Shortly after Lester's graduation from high school, Uncle Charles used his connections to get him a job at the automobile plant he worked at. At twenty-one, Lester married his high school sweetheart and took up residence in the suburbs. My youngest sister Deb got pregnant at fourteen, gave birth at fifteen, and got engaged at seventeen. With her boyfriend and one-year-old daughter Hope, she moved into a two-family house. Remaining at home were my mother, baby brother, and myself. With everyone else gone, I did my best to help Mom with Mario. In fact, he was with me so much, people started thinking he was mine.

I focused on getting myself together, so *I* could move out of the projects. Briefly, I worked as an elevator operator at upscale Cleveland Plaza Hotel. With great pride, I wore my navy jacket-and-skirt uniform and ran elevator number one. I liked the job and my coworkers, four older females who looked out for me. As well I enjoyed meeting people from all over the world. But even though my work received praise from my supervisor, the job ended abruptly after only seven months. A recently hired man from my neighborhood went to the supervisor and informed her, "Connie's not a real girl." I was fired on the spot. Humiliated and angry, I questioned why it mattered if I conducted myself professionally.

Out of work, a twice-weekly drama workshop at Karamu House kept me busy. As part of a plan to completely cross over into mainstream society as Connie (I destroyed most pictures of me

My Journey to Me

taken before 1971), past associates were dropped, with the exception of my best friend Jackie Carson. As a result, I had no social life, except when Jackie came home from college (She had transferred from University of Cincinnati to Columbia in New York). There was no boyfriend either. I wasn't even dating. My last date had been a year earlier with a wrong number. I was trying to dial my mother from a friend's house but reached an Anthony "Tony" Jones instead. Except for the last digit, the numbers were identical. After apologizing, I hung up and retried. "Is Mama there?"

"You dialed *me* again," Tony chuckled.

"Oh, I'm sorry. It's just that the numbers are so similar."

"That's okay," he said. Then he hung up. My third "misdial" was no mistake. Tony struck up a conversation. "You have a nice voice. Do you look like you sound? You're not, well, big, are you?" He laughed.

"I look just fine," I assured him. I liked his voice also, especially the warm laughter. After a pleasant half-hour conversation, mostly about our preferences in music, I gave him my number. He called the following evening and we talked for about an hour, again, mostly about music. After talking over the phone every day for a week, he asked me out.

"Would you like to go to dinner tomorrow evening?"

"Yeah, I'd love to," I answered.

"What kind of food do you like?"

"Anything but Italian and Mexican. Too spicy."

"Yeah, same here. Pick you up at seven?"

"How about seven-thirty?"

Tony arrived twenty minutes early the following evening. I was quite pleased when I answered the door. Suited in dark green, about five-nine, dark and attractive with a close beard and good manners, Tony had a maturity that extended beyond his twenty years. Our first date was at a swank downtown restaurant. A gentleman, Tony opened doors for me and pulled back my chair. Conversation was steady and entertaining, mostly about dreams for the future and our mutual love for vintage jazz. I wasn't the least bit surprised when he asked for a second date. The following evening we went to a drive-in movie to see *The Mack* and had an even better time than the night before. Over the next two weeks we got along remarkably well. We talked on the phone every day and went out to eat every other day. Then I made the mistake of asking to borrow twenty dollars. "I don't lend money," Tony said as he looked away.

Insulted and somewhat embarrassed, I asked, "Why not?'
"Why not? I just don't!"
A minor disagreement escalated to me calling him a "cheap creep!" and Tony storming out the door. He hadn't called since. Out of loneliness and boredom, I called *him*, almost a year later.

"Hi, Tony, this is um—Connie."
"Yeah?" he answered
"Um—would you like to go to the movies?"
"No, I wouldn't but . . ."
"Oh, okay then. Bye."
"No, wait! You didn't give me a chance to finish. I don't want to go to the movies but I'd like to take you to dinner, if that's okay."
"Dinner would be great," I said—relieved.

Tony started our date with an apology. "Hey, I'm real sorry about what happened the last time I saw you."

"It's forgotten," I assured him and quickly changed the subject. I wasn't proud of my part in the disagreement either. At one of the best restaurants in town we dined on lobster, drank far too much champagne, and danced till closing. By the end of the romantic evening we were a couple. Nothing specific was said. We just knew.

Tony was too high and tired to drive home. "Would it be okay if I spent the night at your place?" he asked.

"Of course," I replied. But even though he stayed the night, nothing sexual happened. We just slept in each other's arms, exhausted from the evening. Not "ready" to be intimate yet, I never got totally nude. I wasn't too self-conscious about my small breasts but always wore panties, even when alone. Revealing my gender problem to Tony (or anyone else who didn't already know) was out of the question. My genitalia painlessly tucked inside my body, if he rubbed against or touched between my legs, he would feel what appeared to be the small mound of a vagina. I didn't feel at the time that I was deceiving him so much as I was protecting myself. I had trusted a guy before and was open about my problem. He seemed understanding and even offered words of compassion. Later I found out he told everyone he knew and in the most negative way possible. After trusting others and getting the same result, I decided to protect myself and give people a chance to get to know me first, uninfluenced by prejudices. If they found out later, I figured they could "judge" me as the person I was, and not as some kind of abomination. I wasn't going to lessen my options in life or be thought of as some sort of freak.

Tony left my place for work early that following morning. After work he went home, showered, changed, and returned to my house. It became his daily routine. Mom didn't mind Tony practically living at our place. She thought of him as a "good catch." But after a month *Tony* suggested, "Let's get our own space. We're too old to still be living with our parents." He was twenty-one; I was twenty.

I was nervous the first time Tony took me to meet his parents. Mr. Jones, a friendly and outspoken man, believed in hard work and making money. He prided himself on owning "some of the best-maintained apartment buildings in the inner city." Having recently become Republican, he loved talking politics, especially about anything to do with the Democrats. "Democrats never did anything for me!" he complained. "As hard as I use to work for them." Tony looked like his mother, a slender, dark-skinned lady of few words and some skepticism about the new girlfriend.

When Tony blurted out, "Guess what, I'm moving!" I cringed.

A church-going Christian, Mrs. Jones asked, "Shouldn't you be married first?"

Before Tony could answer I said, "Mrs. Jones, your home is beautifully decorated. May I see the rest of it." I liked the Joneses and the feeling seemed mutual. There was just the matter of Tony and me living together, unmarried.

After living in a rental in Bedford Heights for a year, Tony purchased a townhouse for us on Dalebridge Road in Warrensville Heights. I was deliriously happy and took the role of suburban housewife seriously. Tony came in from work every day to a spotless house, home-cooked meal, and immaculately groomed "wife." I decorated with antiques, oriental artwork, and lots of crystal, like I had seen in the pages of *House and Garden*. We had pets as well: an Afghan hound named Phillip and four exotic birds.

Things couldn't have been better financially. Tony had just been promoted on his job from apprentice to journeyman glazier. Having worked since his teens he also had over ten thousand dollars saved as well as excellent credit and no outstanding bills. After teaching me to drive, he bought me a powder blue 1967 Mercedes Benz. He purchased a dark green '72 Benz for himself. Tony also presented me with my very own credit card. "Buy whatever you need," he said. "Just try not to get carried away." At seventy-five percent off sales, I purchased a closet-full of designer fashions. When I landed a leading role in a Karamu House production of "Crucificado," Tony rewarded me with a diamond ring with matching earrings totaling four and a half carats—wholesale, of course. I felt blessed. Not long ago I was broke and living in the projects. More importantly, I had someone who wanted to share his life with me.

My "husband" and I shared many things in common, including our appreciation for music. He *lived* for jazz, especially sax players like Charlie Parker, Coleman Hawkins, and John Coltrane, while I favored vocalists like Billie Holliday, Sarah Vaughn, and Ella Fitzgerald. "Since we both love music, why don't we learn to play instruments?" Tony suggested. Then he bought a tenor sax for him and a piano for me. Over the next two years I studied classical piano and even played in two recitals. Along with my sister Deb, who was learning to play the clarinet, Tony and I played together every Sunday afternoon—except when Tony and I stayed out too late the night before.

Dormant for way too long, my social life started to pick up. Tony had a cousin, a doctor who welcomed me into her circle of young black professionals. We took turns hosting parties, given on an average of once a month. The best were the yearly bashes held at her Cleveland Heights mansion. They were one of the most anticipated events in town and attracted the crème de la crème of young black professionals. My older sister Ernestine, recently divorced, met her second spouse at one of those parties.

With an active social life and a comfortable home life, Tony and I were blissfully happy—or so I thought. After nearly two years together, he started to become distant, almost cordial. When confronted, he merely said, "Things just aren't working out."

"What do you mean?" I asked. "I thought things were perfect! You hadn't indicated that you were anything but happy! What happened? Your mother?"

Mrs. Jones was constantly trying to run Tony's life, hitting him with questions like: "Why do you have to live in the suburbs

She Can Go Where Pretty Girls Go

instead of the city? Why do you have to have foreign cars instead of domestic? When are you going to get married?" She also felt I should have a job. To me, cooking, cleaning, washing, handling the household budget, and running all the errands was a job.

"Besides what kind of job could I get without a high school diploma?" I thought. Pitifully, I tried to reason with Tony. "Honey, can't we just work out whatever problems there are?"

He shrugged and answered, "I don't know. I just don't know." Then he retired to the bedroom.

"What am I suppose to do now?" I wondered. "And what if he actually breaks up with me?" I had built my very existence around our lives together. Having come too far to go back to the projects, I had to think of a way to earn some money—just in case.

While browsing through the latest issue of *Vogue*, I came across a beautifully done Yves Saint-Laurent spread. The designer's opulent off-the-shoulder peasant blouses and long flowing skirts were both romantic and inspirational. Lost in the pages, I came up with an idea. "What if I gave a fashion show?" I immediately phoned my sister for her opinion.

"I love it!" said Deb. "In fact, I'd like to help." The more we talked, the more convinced I became we could do it.

"We could follow up the show with a disco," I said. The entire world had gone disco in 1976.

"Well; what are we waiting for?" Deb wanted to know. "Let's go for it!"

Needing the perfect spot, we chose The Theatrical, an upscale restaurant located downtown. Tony and I had dined there often. The food was good and they featured live jazz. Deb and I met with the manager and pitched our idea. "Our crowd will be upscale," we assured him, "and we'll advertise the starting time as two hours prior to the show to give our people ample time to dine in your restaurant." He nodded his head slowly. "We also propose a cash bar", guaranteeing the restaurant that a certain amount of alcoholic beverages will be purchased. He loved that idea. Our profits would come solely from ticket sales, but we were confident we could sell the five hundred tickets, priced at fifteen dollars in advance, twenty at the door. Smiling, the manager led us upstairs to an elegant ballroom where our event would be held. It was perfect. With both parties satisfied, we shook hands. The restaurant was guaranteed a full house and we got the place for practically nothing.

Inspired by the romantic spring collection of Yves Saint-Laurent, Deb and I dubbed the event "A Spring Romance." We had flyers and tickets printed up. Advertisement started by word of mouth. We told our friends who told their friends and so on. I convinced two disc jockeys to mention our event on the radio, free of charge. In the evenings Deb and I got dolled up and hit every upscale club and party in town to pass out flyers and hype the show. Much of the day was spent actually putting the show together.

We enlisted a local dressmaker as the show's designer and borrowed additional clothing from area shops. Music would be provided by a disc jockey. I chose to supervise the backstage and Tony was put in charge of collecting money and tickets at the door. With her calm demeanor and gracious manner, Deb would make the perfect hostess. Also, needing twelve models, three white girls were recruited from a Barbizon School of Modeling—at no cost because the girls needed experience and pictures for their portfolios. They were *terrible* on the runway, so rehearsals were scheduled. I figured I could coach them, even though my only experience consisted of an hour-long class at Artha Jon's School of Modeling at age sixteen. Along with the Barbizon girls I recruited seven girlfriends and two aspiring actors from Karamu House. The show's commentator was from there as well.

She Can Go Where Pretty Girls Go

My best friend Jackie Carson, who flew in from New York to help "ensure the quality of the show," came into modeling rehearsals and completely took over. Brutally honest in critiquing the models, she shouted, "Their walking is horrible!" and proceeded to demonstrate how it should be done. She exaggeratedly dipped and spun as she strutted down an imaginary runway, freezing in place for the occasional pose. The models hated her!

"Who does she think *she* is?" one snapped.

"This is *your* show!" another reminded me. I appreciated Jackie's help, understood her sense of professionalism, and agreed with most of her criticisms, but felt she was being harsh.

"Time's running out and they need to be ready!" said Jackie. Hesitantly, I agreed and let her carry on, hoping the models wouldn't strut their stuff—right out the door.

The models never quite mastered the art of runway walking during rehearsals, and after five weeks of nonstop activity, the day of the big show arrived. Tony looked dashing in a three-piece Pierre Cardin suit: Deb and I wore billowy tops with straight knee-length skirts and strapped satin heels. On our way to the restaurant, we prayed that all our advertising and promotions would pay off. Although most of the tickets had been sold and a profit already made, we still needed people to pay at the door. We wanted to make as much money as possible.

We arrived at The Theatrical an hour and a half before show time. The restaurant was filled with our guests, dining as they listened to the sounds of the Freddy Cole Trio. After speaking to a few friends, Tony, Deb, and I walked upstairs to the ballroom to find the models, disc jockey, and backstage personnel had all arrived. The runway and backstage had been set up the previous day. Jackie was backstage organizing clothing and adding accessories. There were only three people to help twelve models with very fast changes: her, the show's designer, and me.

My Journey to Me

I was overjoyed by the turnout. Over five hundred people showed up, dressed "casual evening" as the flyers and tickets dictated. Most had come from dining downstairs and were having cocktails and socializing while Tony's collection of vintage jazz played softly in the background.

Everyone silenced when the commentator announced the beginning of the fashion show. "Ladies and gentlemen, I'd like to welcome you to A Spring Romance." The models did on the runway what most were unable to do in rehearsals—walk! Serving major attitude, they strutted like they were on a catwalk on New York's Seventh Avenue. We opened with casual wear featuring oversized off-the-shoulder blouses with long full skirts. Ultrasuede suits, pants, and dresses followed. During the sportswear segment our only male model surprised everyone (including me) by peeling off his peach velour sweat suit down to skimpy bulging swim trunks. The ladies in the audience stood and screamed. A female model followed in a bikini that covered only her nipples and most of her crotch.

One male spectator who obviously had too much to drink yelled, "Take it off, I'll help!" as embarrassed friends shushed.

We ended the show with sexy eveningwear, party music, tons of confetti, and a standing ovation. I was extremely proud of everyone. The backstage people were quick, the models inventive, and the music right on cue. Following the show, the tables and chairs were quickly resituated and the room magically transformed into a disco.

After we danced three straight songs, a very proud Tony grabbed hold of my hand and led me backstage. "I apologize for being such a jerk," he said. "I don't want you ever to leave me. I love you." Then he kissed me, passionately. "A Spring Romance" turned out to be the party of the season and a big financial success. It certainly put the spring back in our romance.

As we celebrated our second anniversary at home with a romantic candlelight dinner, I thought of how frustrating it must have been for Tony, not having sex. It certainly was for me since intimacy consisted mostly of hugging and hunching. I still hadn't revealed my gender problem to Tony. "How would I tell him?" I thought. "And what would he think of me?" I wouldn't want him to think of me as gay, or as a drag queen. I had nothing against queens; I just wasn't one. People often file transsexuals in the gay category without even having any knowledge on the subject. I thought of myself as having a birth defect. My body didn't match my psyche. It was impossible to change my psyche, so a small part of my body would have to be altered. It was the best way I knew how to explain it. Doctors explained it as a disorder that occurs in the endocrine glands.

I had been in the gender disorder program at University Hospital for three years. Initially accepted in Metropolitan Hospital's program (back in 1972), when I was eighteen, I didn't meet the minimum age requirement of twenty-one. Metropolitan placed me on a waiting list with plans to schedule my surgery when I became of age. Meanwhile, over the next two years, I had session after session with social workers and psychologists, and every physical examination possible. When I became disillusioned with the program (because of my lack of faith in the doctors and the bad results of one of their first patients) I applied to and was accepted into University Hospital's program. Meeting twice weekly with psychologist Dr. Leslie Lothstein, for the first time in my life I got a chance to freely discuss things held guarded inside. The doctor seemed to really care about the intimate details of my life. In fact, he seemed fascinated. After over three long years in the program I was finally given a surgery date.

My patience had worn paper-thin over the years. At twenty-four, I was eager to get the procedure done so I could get on

My Journey to Me

with my life. Urologist Dr. Elroy Kursh was to perform the surgery. I had been his patient for over three years and had the utmost confidence in him. Then a problem arose, adding to the already long delay. A surgery date was scheduled at University but a riff between Dr. Kursh and the hospital developed and they refused to allow him to operate there. The doctor asked me, "Please be patient a little longer and don't lose confidence in me. I promise to find another hospital soon." Meanwhile, University phoned to tell me that even though Dr. Kursh was no longer with the hospital I could still have my surgery, but that a different doctor would be doing it. At that point I was beyond desperate to get everything over with but declined their offer. My surgery was far too important to entrust to a stranger. Knowing Dr. Kursh was supposed to do it, I waited. He phoned three agonizing months later, with the news. "Ready for your surgery? We got an admittance date."

"Really?" I asked.

"Yes. For real this time."

"Great!" I shouted. "Finally! Doctor, thank you so much!" I hung up, bowed my head, and just wept. Obviously because I was happy, but also because it had taken so damn *long*!

I explained to Tony that I was going in the hospital for minor "female problems," the excuse I had given since the beginning to explain why we weren't having a complete sex life. I assured him the operation would fix the problem. Tony was patient and supportive. He paid for the expensive Blue Cross-Blue Shield insurance and helped fatten me up so I'd be strong for the procedure.

On the day of my scheduled operation in early 1977, Cleveland experienced a horrific blizzard. Heavy snow and powerful icy winds brought traffic to a near halt and shut down electrical power in most of the city. The power was out at Mt. Sinai Hospital, which was operating on emergency generators. Sitting on a

She Can Go Where Pretty Girls Go

gurney, prepped and waiting to be rolled into the operating room, I asked the attending nurse, "How can my surgery be performed without electricity?" She shrugged. I feared the operation would once again be postponed. Just as I began to seriously doubt, Dr. Kursh stormed in.

"Don't worry," he said. "I'm going to perform your operation, power outage or not!" Then he left. He returned a half-hour later with some good though somewhat disturbing news. "I'm going ahead with the operation, but we're going to have to use the hospital's backup generator."

"Is that going to be okay?" I asked.

"It'll be better than okay," he answered confidently. After years of waiting I was finally on the operating table, drugged and trying to count backwards as ordered by the doctor.

"One hundred, ninety-nine, ninetyyyy."

I woke to a blurred face and muffled reassuring female voice. "The operation went perfectly and you're now in the recovery room." Still extremely groggy, I drifted back off. When I woke up in a private room, there was Tony's concerned face watching over me.

"You okay?" he asked.

"Yeah," I whispered, "just numb. And drugged." I slowly turned my head to look in a mirror and gasped when I saw tubes running from my body to who knows where. After a few incoherent words, I passed out. When I woke up Tony was gone.

Immobility, pain, nurses from hell, and a gray view buried in snow plunged me into depression. All I could do was lie there, close to tears, staring at a large brown spot on the floor. "They *need* to sweep this nasty room," I thought. "Wait! Did that spot *move?*" I was so drugged I wasn't sure. When it started crawling, I realized it wasn't a spot at all, but a huge cockroach! Unable to move, I panicked. "What if I got an infection?" I thought. I screamed for the nurse and pressed out a distress signal on my bedside buzzer. Two black nurses rushed into the room. The tall skinny sounded agitated.

"What's all the commotion about?" she asked.

"There's a huge nasty roach in my room!" I answered. The short heavyset one chuckled.

"A roach? Is that all, chile? Shoot, they got mice up on Ten!" Relieved there was no real emergency, they left.

Getting more depressed each day, I focused all my energy on recovering quickly. Tony brought in food daily from outside. I received several phone calls but only had one other visitor, my sister Ernestine. My best friend Jackie was away at school. My sister Deb didn't even know I was in the hospital. She had moved to Atlanta, Georgia, two months earlier and I had yet to hear from her. I planned to track her down as soon as I got out of the hospital. Gratefully, my physical recovery was fast and I was released after only nine days. (There would be two more operations before the year was out.) Dr. Kursh did an amazing job. I was thankful to have been delivered into his capable hands.

Tony and I couldn't wait. We made love even before I got the go-ahead from my doctor. The first time was very romantic. Seated on the bedroom sofa, excited and a little nervous, we sipped champagne by candlelight while Marvin Gaye serenaded from the downstairs stereo. Tony removed his pajama bottoms, my camisole and panties, then placed me gently on the bed. Lying on top he began kissing me. "I love you," he said softly. Then he parted my legs and slowly entered. I trembled then moaned.

"It's my first time," I whispered in his ear. He was gentle at first, as he slowly moved in and out, each stroke more amazing than the last. Then he started grinding; faster; harder. Soon he was humping so hard, at one point I thought the bed might collapse. Excited to the point of nearly blacking out, I clawed into his back until, to my

She Can Go Where Pretty Girls Go

joy and amazement, I reached an orgasm, an explosion of a million short sweet bursts. Tony moaned as he came immediately afterwards. Then we collapsed in each other's arms until he fell fast asleep. Overjoyed my vagina was functional I was still awake and smiling hours later—and ready to do it again.

Although my operation was a success, a year after my third and final surgery, I was still depressed, convinced I was dying. A constant ringing in my ears and persistent neck pain made each day hell. I saw twelve different doctors, but none could diagnose my problem. Finally I made an appointment with my psychologist Dr. Lothstein, who I hadn't seen since before going into the hospital. "Postsurgical shock," he diagnosed. "Having three major operations over such a short period of time was a tremendous burden on your body *and* your mind."

Tony became concerned about my declining emotional state and suggested, "Why don't you visit your friend Jackie in New York?" I loved the idea and so did Jackie. Tired of doctors and hospitals, I was ready for some fun.

I had a fabulous time from the moment my plane landed at LaGuardia. Jackie lived with her boyfriend of three years in a two-bedroom apartment on 107th and Fifth Avenue. She was also attending Columbia University, majoring in economics. "Girl, I am so glad you're here," she said. "I haven't been doing anything but going to school and it's getting *sickening!*"

"And I'm tired of doctors and hospitals," I replied. "I'm ready to have some fun." And we did. We went to the Metropolitan Museum, had afternoon cocktails at the Stork Club, shopped at Bloomingdales, and had one really big night on the town. Jackie's friend Sheila Phillips was company manager for the Broadway production, *Your Arms Too Short to Box with God*, and invited us as her guests. Afterwards we went to Harlem's legendary Cotton Club for cocktails and jazz, then later to Studio 54 for a wild

My Journey to Me

and wonderful night of partying at what was the hottest disco on the planet in the late seventies. I had never seen anything like it! Celebrities and beautiful people of all races and sexual preferences drinking, drugging, and dancing the night away. Toward the end of the evening, or should I say early morning, a giant half-moon with a coke spoon lodged up its nose descended from the high ceiling as confetti and fake snow showered the dancers. Partying at Studio 54 was the perfect ending to a fantastic visit.

I had a wonderful time in New York but it felt good to be back home with Tony. The trip did the trick. I was no longer depressed. In fact I felt happy: grateful for my health, a resolution to my gender problem, and a husband who adored me. Life seemed perfect, but unfortunately nothing ever is.

The economic climate was getting bad in Cleveland. Work was so slow that Tony's company assigned him a job in Detroit, Michigan. He worked there during the week and came home on the weekend. Even though I missed him I couldn't complain, grateful he was still working. Many weren't. Although we spoke over the phone every evening, I was always anxious for his return on the weekends.

On one particular Friday evening I was more anxious than usual to see Tony. Aside from missing him, we were having a party the following day and I needed his help. He always phoned as soon as he got off work to let me know he was on his way. The call never came. Tony usually got home around eight. By ten I became concerned and phoned his mother. She hadn't heard from him either. I called again at twelve but there was still no word. I waited and worried. By dawn my worrying had mutated into seething anger, recalling what I had heard other women say about married men who stayed out all night. "All men cheat!"

My response had always been, "Not mine!"

She Can Go Where Pretty Girls Go

When I saw the look on Tony's face when he finally came strutting in at eleven o'clock in the morning, I knew instantly what had happened. "I was too exhausted to drive in all that heavy traffic," he said, the pitch of his voice rising with each lying syllable. "I spent the night alongside the highway waiting for traffic to let up." I was so angry, without so much as a word, I snatched the phone from the table and hurled it. It sounded a loud thump against his shoulder just as I leaped on top of him.

"How could you?" I screamed. Then I ran upstairs, threw myself across the bed, and starting bawling. I never imagined Tony would cheat on me. "It just doesn't make sense," I thought. "When we *weren't* having sex, he was faithful. Now that we're *having* sex, he cheats?"

Still in tears when Tony came into the bedroom, I made him admit to the affair. "I'm so sorry," he said. "I don't know what made me do it. It wasn't serious and I swear, it only happened one time."

"I'm leaving you if you're not going to be honest," I threatened.

"Okay," he said nervously. "Okay. Well, she lived in the um—projects where I was working."

"The projects?"

"Yeah."

"Go on."

"She's a single welfare mother with four kids."

"What?" Insult and confusion were added to my hurt and anger. I had worked hard to become the chic suburban housewife and he had an affair with a welfare mother from the projects???

Then he had the nerve to say, "You're always so perfect, you sometimes make me feel like I'm not good enough for you. She made me feel important."

"So you're saying it's *my* fault you fucked her? That's bullshit!" I yelled. "You could have come to me with your grievances instead of jumping in bed with somebody else!" While I listened on an extension, I made him phone the girl and call her horrible names so he wouldn't be able to see her again. It was a desperate attempt on my part to make everything feel right again. "You won't be going to Detroit or on any other out-of-town job assignments without me!" I shouted. I didn't know how to leave Tony. There would have to be a way for him to make it up to me. As difficult as it was, I had to temporarily put the entire mess out of my mind. Fifty guests were expected at my party that evening and there was still plenty to do.

In spite of everything, I was a radiant hostess that night, though I drank more than usual trying to dull the pain. The party got a little wild at times. While most were content boogying to the latest disco hits, some of my more adventurous and drunk guests decided to take a late-night swim (in the pool out back), fully clothed. Then Tony lost his temper because a guest was dancing too provocatively with me and threatened to throw him through the living room window. When it became too noisy for my next door neighbor, a single white teacher in her mid forties, the Warrensville Heights police visited, asking us politely to "keep it down." The party was just what I needed after the day's devastation and became the talk among my guests and me for weeks.

I was wakened the morning after the party with a heartfelt apology from Tony. "I'll do anything in the world to make it up to you, Connie."

"Ummm—what compensation would be enough for me to continue living with a man who had violated my love, trust, and respect?" I wondered. It didn't take long to come up with something. Something I had wanted for a long time. The following weekend we went to shop for my compensation gift, a fabulous full-length ranch mink by Saga Furs, the most gorgeous thing I had ever seen. But as beautiful as the gift was, it couldn't compensate for the loss of trust.

Tony went even further in trying to appease me. "Let's get married," he said. His timing was way off. When I didn't jump at that idea, he proposed something else to win back my trust. "I want to have legal papers drawn up so you'll be provided for if something happened to me or we broke up." If either of us dissolved the relationship I would be entitled to a fourth of his earnings for the length of time we were together. The contract would also state my entitlement to half of everything he owned. When we went to a lawyer, we were told that the contract wasn't necessary, that common-law marriages were recognized in Ohio, and that I was already entitled to whatever my husband earned or owned. Tony still insisted on the contract as a show of faith. We both signed the document and it did make me feel just a little more secure within the "marriage." Slowly Tony regained my trust. It also helped that he never cheated again.

After the cheating incident I felt *I* should be more honest with *Tony*. "How can I expect total trust from him when I'm not being totally honest myself," I thought. That's when I told him my secret. "I'm sorry I didn't tell you sooner," I said. "I just couldn't!" In shock, he didn't speak; he just stared at me.

Then, slowing shaking his head, he said, "I just find it hard to believe. Is this some kind of bad joke?"

"I'm afraid not. I'm so sorry, Tony. There were many times I wanted to tell you. I just didn't know how."

"I need to get out of here for a minute. I need to think," he said. Then he left. I just sat on the sofa and waited nervously. When Tony returned about twenty-five minutes to half an hour later, he embraced me. "I don't care about the past," he whispered. "You're every bit a woman and my wife." Feeling a tremendous weight had been lifted and grateful Tony still loved me,

I cried. Gradually we grew close again and tried settling back into our life, pre-affair and pre-confession. But hard economic times would make that nearly impossible.

Steel mills and automobile plants were doing massive layoffs or shutting down altogether. Cleveland's economy depended heavily on those industries. Construction came to a near halt and Tony, along with thousands of other workers, was laid off. With a mortgage to pay, we had to do something fast. Tony had heard that jobs in his field were plentiful in Houston, Texas, which was being called a boomtown. "Hey, nothing's going on here and I have to do something," he said. "What would you think about moving to Texas?"

"Heee hawww!" I hollered. After renting our house to my sister Deb (who had since moved back from Atlanta, Georgia), we packed up our belongings and took a flight to Houston with no idea of what to expect.

We arrived at Houston's Intercontinental Airport in September of 1981. Unbearably hot and humid with a terrain so flat it seemed enveloped by the sky, magnificent skyscrapers in all futuristic sizes and shapes were springing up all over the place. Elevated freeways running straight through the city were congested with an onslaught of modern-day pioneers who had come from all over the world to take advantage of opportunities in the rapidly growing metropolis.

Tony found employment immediately and the pay was even better than in Cleveland. We made our nest amongst the skyscrapers downtown. Our thirtieth-story penthouse apartment at the Houston House was impressive, offering maid service, a dry cleaner, lounge, supermarket, indoor garage with twenty-four hour security, and a concierge. On the tenth floor were two swimming pools and a fully equipped weight room with a magnificent view of downtown.

She Can Go Where Pretty Girls Go

Houston re-energized me, gave me hope, some ambition. Even though Tony was generous, I felt I at least needed to be able to support myself. The first step would be getting formally educated. I had been too ashamed to tell Tony I hadn't finished high school. After my confession, I told him I wanted to get my high school equivalency diploma, then go to college. He gave his full support. At age twenty-nine, after receiving a General Equivalency Diploma, I entered Texas Southern University, majoring in communications. Tony was so proud when I made the dean's list my first semester there and became the early-morning newscaster for KTSU, the school radio station.

Over the next three years I was happier than ever. Besides doing well in school, tropical-like climate, and new friends, Tony and I were getting along better than ever. There was also MTV, an exciting and revolutionary new television station that rotated music video clips of the latest hit songs. When not studying I watched, waiting for Michael Jackson's "Billie Jean" and Prince's "Little Red Corvette." Intrigued, I thought, "It sure would be exciting to work in the music industry." In the rejuvenating atmosphere of Houston everything seemed possible. Then the great boom went bust and things changed, seemingly overnight. Tony began to work less and less, eventually getting laid off altogether. With less money, our relationship became strained. Tony spent hours every day pacing, his nerves on edge—putting my nerves on edge. Luckily, Tony's unemployment only lasted four months. The economy was picking up back in Cleveland and his old job wanted him back. "But what am I going to do about school?" I asked. "I only have a year and a half left before I get my degree."

"I'm sorry, but you can't stay," said Tony. "I just can't afford it." That was that. Since I was in the middle of a school semester, we decided I would stay until classes were over. Tony had to leave for Cleveland immediately.

My Journey to Me

At the end of the fall semester Tony returned to move all our belongings and me back to Cleveland. I hated leaving. It had been my plan to finish my education at TSU and afterwards work in Los Angeles, possibly as a newscaster. "I'm definitely not moving to LA," said Tony. "I might consider New York. You could maybe go up and get situated and I could come later. There're plenty of jobs in my field there and I prefer it to LA because it's closer to Cleveland. And I could visit you on weekends until I moved up."

"Are you sure?" I asked. I didn't like New York enough to live there without Tony, but there were too few employment opportunities for me in Cleveland. Tony also reminded me that my best friend lived in New York.

When I ran the idea by Jackie she loved it. She had graduated from Columbia University with a degree in Economics but chose to become a makeup artist and promote fragrances for Estee Lauder at Bloomingdales'. She had been feeling "a little down" since she and her boyfriend broke up. They had a four-year-old daughter together, making it even more difficult. But Jackie said she was ready to pick up with her life and move on. It was settled. Tony and I agreed I would stay in New York until he could save more money and join me later. I used money from my savings for our move from Houston, back to Cleveland. I planned to spend the 1984 Christmas holiday in Cleveland, then go to New York.

She Can Go Where Pretty Girls Go

Tony (right) and me dressed for a night out on the town: 1974.

My Journey to Me

Me at twenty-one-years old.

A NEW LIFE

Tony and I arrived in New York City at dawn in a small rented van, packed to capacity with most of my possessions. We were startled when we entered Jackie's apartment. She had mentioned she was feeling "a little down" and that the apartment was "a little disheveled." What we found was far worse: Jackie seemed depressed, and the place was a total mess. A birdcage sat on the floor near the bathroom with its ill-tempered occupant, Rodney, perched on top. Next to it stood a large mound of discarded sunflower seed shells. I gagged, trying not to throw up, after I swept into the pile and a horde of roaches swarmed out. Jackie had recently purchased another pet, a Pekingnese. "I've wanted one for years because they're tres chic," she said. Since the apartment complex didn't allow pets, she rarely took the dog out. Theoretically he was to do his business out on the terrace and presumably Jackie would clean it up. But not only was dog do-do on the terrace, it was right in the middle of the living room floor! Dog pee as well! My two almost-new salmon sofas, brought to replace Jackie's old one, were treated like fire hydrants. Ruined!

A New Life

All of a sudden Cleveland didn't look so bad. "I change my mind about staying in New York," I told Tony. But his response wasn't exactly what I wanted to hear.

"You've only been here for a few days. Since we've gone through all the trouble and expense of moving your things here, you might as well give it a shot. If you want to come home after a month, when we can better afford yet another move, you can. Besides, your friend looks like she could use your help."

"Yeah, but who's going to help me?" I asked.

"Me!" answered Tony. "I'll stay a couple more days and help get the place cleaned up. Please be patient and give me a chance to save some money." Sadly, after four days of trying to help get the apartment *and* me in order, Tony left for Cleveland.

The only thing that kept me together was the thought; "I won't be here long."

I phoned Tony every evening for three weeks with the same greeting: "I want to come home!"

"Hang in there a little while longer," was his usual response.

"Please, Honey. I'm having a *horrible* time and you're not even sending enough money." Not even tears softened his stance.

"Just be patient a little while longer and I'll come and get you," he promised. But I was tired of waiting on Tony and decided to find a job and *earn* the money for my move home.

Sheila Phillips was a friend of Jackie whom I had met during a prior visit to the city. Previously a production manager for scores of Broadway plays, she had recently opened her own business, Broadway Tix, offering theatre packages at discounted rates. "Business is booming!" said Sheila before inviting me to join her staff of five as a sales agent. I gladly accepted. The office was located in the same theatre where Harvey Fierstein was starring in the Broadway smash, *Torch Song Trilogy*. Besides answering phones, taking orders, and soliciting clients, it was my job to pick up and deliver tickets and money to and from various Broadway theatres. One of the company's bigger sellers was the off-Broadway gospel musical *Mama I Want to Sing*, a favorite among church groups across black America.

A month and three weeks crawled by and once again I was on the phone with Tony discussing my return to Cleveland. Once again he suggested I remain in New York, "especially since you just started a new job." I suspected something was wrong. Tony was becoming more evasive when I talked about returning home and his phone calls slacked off considerably. *I* was the one who usually called.

Finally, I said point blank, "I'm coming home. You won't have to spend a dime. I've saved a few dollars." His unenthusiastic reaction to my good news wasn't exactly what I expected.

In a cold, detached voice my "husband" of ten years said, "I don't want you to come back. Why don't you just stay there?" My body went limp. He followed the blow with a feeble attempt to justify his actions. "You're responsible for me owing a couple of thousand in taxes."

Struggling to remain calm, I reminded him, "It's your unqualified uncle who prepares your taxes, not me."

When he repeated, "You should stay in New York," I lost it and cursed him with every foul word I could think of. He hung up on me. I called right back but he wouldn't answer. Our next conversation the following night ended in a terrible argument and another hang-up. When I called the next day the number had been changed, and was unlisted. The rejection was unbearable. All I could do was bury my face in my hands and cry. Being abandoned in New York was bad enough; being left penniless was overwhelming. Having used my savings for living expenses in Houston my last few months there, as well as moving expenses from Houston to Cleveland to New York, I was left with only fifty

A New Life

dollars and a shattered promise. After ten years together, the most important person in my life was gone. Not only was I devastated, I felt doublecrossed!

I had two options. I could return to Cleveland where I had no job or place to live and wage a legal battle for the house and temporary financial support. That would cost money, which I didn't have, and there was always the possibility I could lose. My second option was to remain in New York where I at least had a friend, a job, and a place to stay. There were limitless opportunities in Manhattan. I just had to take advantage of them.

A better paying job was essential if I was going to afford my half of the rent and put something aside to move with later. My two-hundred-and-something dollar a week check from Broadway Tix barely got me through the week. When the "Great White Way" fell on dark times (seemingly overnight) and theatre attendance drastically dropped, Sheila's business suffered and I was let go. Thank goodness for my jewelry, which I sold to temporarily sustain myself. The only piece I kept was a two and a half-carat, five-diamond cluster that got stuck on my finger when I accidentally slammed it in the closet door. Luckily, I wasn't unemployed for long. When a friend called about an opening in the Garment District, I interviewed and got the job. My position as administrative assistant to the president of Diane Von Furstenburg Blouses also required me to do some showroom modeling. Although I made a little more money I was still barely surviving.

Barely surviving and missing Tony and my old life, I was miserable. Jackie, on the other hand, was recovering from her depression. She began cleaning again, enrolled her daughter in private school, and returned to work promoting fragrances at Bloomingdales. Just a few months later she opened a lingerie shop at Herald Center Mall called Jacquelyn for Lingerie. There was also

She Can Go Where Pretty Girls Go

a new man in her life: an Italian-American teacher from Queens. It was wonderful to see Jackie happy, laughing again, going out practically every weekend. It wasn't so wonderful that I had become the exact opposite: sad, lonely, and withdrawn. "Girl, get out of this house and have some fun!" Jackie insisted. "You've got to face the fact that Tony is gone!"

"Yeah, but it's just so hard to believe. I thought he would at least care about my well-being," I said.

"He's gone!" Jackie repeated. "Gone! You've got to get on with your life. Go out! Have some fun!" She was right. So busy obsessing over what Tony was or was not going to do, I realized that I hadn't gone out socially since I arrived in New York.

Jackie took me to Sweetwaters, a club she and her new boyfriend frequented. (He was meeting her there later.) Purely by chance I met a man: medium built, brown-skinned, attractive, and very much the gentleman. He had accidentally bumped into me in the crowded bar, spilling my drink. "I'm so sorry. Let me get you another one," he offered.

"Stolyisnaya and tonic with a lime twist," I said as I carefully checked my favorite blouse for damage. He was back in less than a minute with my drink.

"My name is Bas. Is this your first time here?" he asked.

"Yes, it is."

"You like it?"

"Well, it's a little crowded but the music's good and loud."

"Would you like to dance?"

"Oh yeah. That's my song." Everything played seemed to be my song. We danced almost every record. After dancing (and drinking) at the club all night, we breakfasted at La Brasserie (Jackie and her boyfriend went home). I was impressed when Bas picked up the tab for nearly a hundred dollars without batting an eye. Not wanting our time together to end just yet, he suggested, "Let's

A New Life

go to my place for a nightcap." I gladly accepted. It was the most fun I'd had since leaving Houston.

Bas's large studio was sparsely and casually decorated in earth tones and lots of plants—very seventies. We listened to soft music and discussed ourselves over cognac. "I've only been in the city a few months," I began.

"Oh really, where are you from?" he asked.

"Cleveland, Ohio, by way of South Carolina." His eyes lit up.

"South Carolina? Really?"

"Yeah, for real."

"I was born there too, in St. Stephens," he said, "but I've been here since I was eight. A lot of my family is still there, including my mother, who by the way, just turned ninety-nine."

Of West Indian descent, somewhat mysterious, and unmarried with two grown daughters and six grandchildren, Bas was no-nonsense and grounded, though not forthcoming about his age. He looked like he might be in his late forties, but I suspected older because of his evasiveness. An inspector for the New York Transit Authority, Bas worked a second job during the summers as sound engineer for Jazzmobile, a mobile concert that featured the best names in jazz: Dizzy Gillespie, Lou Donaldson, Milt Jackson, Sonny Rollins. Bas made me feel comfortable, like I had known him for years. In some ways he reminded me of Tony because of his frankness, down-to-earthiness, and generosity. In other ways he was totally different. Whereas Tony was sometimes chameleon-like, taking on the personality of whoever was around at the time, Bas was his own man, with his own style. That night at his place was the first time I felt relaxed since arriving in New York. I spent the entire weekend.

When I returned to Jackie's on Sunday afternoon, she answered the door dressed in a beautiful magenta maillot and heels. "Hurry up and get your swimsuit!" she said, "We've been invited to a

She Can Go Where Pretty Girls Go

pool party on Long Island! I also invited an ex-coworker from Bloomingdales. She's really beautiful and seems like a lot of fun. She should be here any minute so hurry, get ready!" I was still getting dressed when her guest arrived, twenty minutes after me. From the moment Jackie introduced us, Kim Reeder and I became friends. I was especially impressed by her confidence.

"There are many 'Kimitations' but only one Miss Kim," she said grandly. I believed her. Twenty-four and drop-dead gorgeous, Kim had a model figure, beautiful tan skin, and golden brown curls cut in a chin-length bob. She was born and raised in a black middle-class neighborhood in Queens and refined at a prestigious boarding school. Her energetic calm, enthusiasm, and off-brand humor was as refreshing and unique as her bohemian twist on fashion (She wore a long oversized print vintage dress over a sexy green bikini). We had a fabulous time at the party, drinking champagne, critiquing men, and laughing at the exact same things. It was a pleasant coincidence to learn that Kim worked right across the street from my job, as receptionist for a knitwear company.

Having a friend who also worked in the Garment District made going to work much more interesting. We lunched in nearby Bryant Park and met after work for drinks, to shop, or simply walk and take in the sights, sounds, and smells of Manhattan. Kim was adventurous and spontaneous. On a moment's notice we could be bowling at Madison Square Garden, dining at a chic restaurant, or sipping champagne in the back of a limousine on our way to a trendy downtown club. "I refuse to let the lack of money prevent me from having or doing what I want," said Kim. "The best in life is mine. I merely have to claim it."

As well as being fun and extremely confident, my new friend was easy to talk to. She told me about her international adventures when she was a flight attendant for Capitol Air. I told her about my previous life with Tony, how we broke up, and how I

A New Life

ended up in New York. "It must be awful, having had so much and having to struggle now," she remarked sympathetically. "What you need to do is get a better paying job and your own apartment."

"Is that a read?" I asked.

"Well, Reeder *is* my last name." she joked. "But seriously," said Kim as she lit a cigarette, "you really do have to get a better paying job and move out."

I had lost interest in my job and was merely going through the motions. The warnings to "Shape up!" went pretty much unheeded, and after working at DVF Blouses for only six months, I was fired. That same day, Kim phoned with some much-needed cheer.

"Congratulations darling, you got press."

"Press?" I asked.

"Your picture's in *Apparel News* magazine."

"Really? How do I look?"

"Fabu (fabulous) of course. A photographer must have snapped you as you were going to or coming from work." I ran out immediately and grabbed five copies. Entitled, "Movers and Shakers," the two-page spread pictured me in a red shaker knit sweater, white skirt, and Armani flats. It was just the bandage my bruised ego needed.

Two weeks after being fired, I landed another job promoting fragrances at Gimbels department store. Work was enjoyable, practically stress-free, and I was making twice as much money. Bored with her job in the Garment District, Kim joined me. It was a blast working together. We were a good selling team and few customers left empty-handed. I did so well, after five months I was offered a manager position, but unfortunately, the store went out of business shortly afterwards.

Out of work, without prospects, Kim and I decided to take a break from everything and just party. For a month, almost nightly we traveled from club to club in limousines with Kim's big-spending pals,

She Can Go Where Pretty Girls Go

some big-time drug dealers. It was Cristal champagne all night long in the VIP rooms of clubs like Area, The Milk Bar, The Tunnel, and Limelight. There was also plenty of cocaine, which I hated because it made me sick. I preferred the calming effects of marijuana.

With Kim almost every day, I hadn't been spending much time with Jackie. Recently, she had moved a new friend into the apartment and the two were becoming inseparable. Jackie's new pal tried to befriend me. Then she started telling me awful things Jackie had supposedly said about me. I assumed she was doing the same thing with Jackie. Rather quickly, my best friend of seventeen years and I became distant, barely speaking. When I told her, "I'm moving out," she quickly responded, "Oh, I was going to have a talk with you about that." It got to a point where I had to move, even though I had no place to go. I didn't want to be a burden on my new friend Kim by asking to stay at her place.

Having spent every weekend at his apartment since we met, I went to see Bas, the only one I felt I could turn to for help. He had been kind and generous, even helping me with rent twice. First I summoned up some courage, then began the story of my living situation, ending with "Can I stay at your place until I get on my feet? It'll only be for a little while, I promise." Bas was sympathetic, but to my surprise, turned me down flat.

"I'm sorry Constance. But it's hard for a bachelor like me to live with anyone."

"Oh, I understand," I said quickly, accepting his answer without too much resentment and quickly pondering another course of action.

Desperate for a place to stay until I figured out what to do, I moved in with a man I had only spoken to a few times at Sweetwaters nightclub. "My stay will be brief," I assured him.

"You can stay as long as you like," he said. There was just one big problem, one thing he neglected to mention. He wanted me

A New Life

there as his girlfriend. Needless to say, the arrangement didn't work out. After fighting off one too many sexual advances, out of sheer desperation I phoned Kim.

"Girl, don't put yourself through," she said. "You can stay with me for a while."

Kim's cozy one-bedroom apartment in downtown Brooklyn was a welcomed change. We enjoyed many hours of laughter and insightful girl chats in her bohemian-decorated living room. An old wood-trimmed sofa for two was covered in pretty print fabric while an antique traveling trunk served as the coffee table. Large Tibetan masks doubled as shades for two urn lamps. Above them hung a framed original by Jean Michel Basquiat. Kim had known the eccentric artist a few years earlier and was presented with one of his works. The relaxing surroundings and Kim's carefree attitude toward life was a refreshing escape from problems of the past several months. Slowly I was starting to enjoy life again.

After living at Kim's for a month, I began to trust and confide in her more. Especially after she commented, "It's so nice having someone to talk to who understands me. Doesn't judge me." During a night of too much champagne I totally opened up and told my secret.

"I wasn't always Constance," I said.

"What do you mean?" asked Kim.

"Well, I wasn't always a girl."

"Are you saying what I *think* you're saying?"

"I was born a boy!" was as direct as I could get. Her mouth flew open.

"You were born *what?*"

"My name was Arlee." I revealed a few more things about my past life as Kim's mouth grew wider with each sentence.

"I don't believe it!" she said. "Cuuute! No, fabbbbulous!" Then she let out a hearty laugh and we hugged. "I love that you trusted

She Can Go Where Pretty Girls Go

me enough to tell me," said Kim. We grew even closer. Even though Kim had a modeling go-see (interview) early the following morning, we spent half the night talking about past lives and dreams for the future.

Kim had started modeling and despised it. "I think it's fucked up that I'm hired solely on my looks! They don't care about how I *feel*, or what I *think*." She went on a video go-see for a new recording group called Levert. They had a single out, "Casanova," and needed a female principal for their debut video. Initially Kim got the part, but the director phoned later to say they were looking for a less sophisticated look and went with a younger girl. She was still paid in full. Kim was also booked to model in designer Oscar de la Renta's bridal show. Dressed in a stunning white lace gown, her picture appeared in the fashion section of the *Daily News* the following day. At the show, Kim met the person responsible for providing the dressers, a black lady named Audrey Smaltz. Thinking of unemployed me, she asked Ms. Smaltz if she needed additional dressers. She gave Kim her card. I called and spoke with Smaltz's assistant Tracy, a soft-spoken lady who took my name, phone number, and referral.

"We'll be calling you soon," she said.

Meanwhile, after six weeks staying at Kim's, I was still unemployed and living off the couple of dollars Bas gave me every week (I still spent weekends there). Even though Kim had stopped paying rent (because of a long-going dispute with the landlord), I felt uncomfortable not being able to contribute much. Then another one of her friends moved in. The place was too small for two people, let alone three. A week after her new roommate's arrival Kim informed him *and* me, "I want my space back." Although hurt and totally unprepared, I didn't hold any ill feelings.

"You're entitled to some privacy," I said. Once again I shoved my pride aside and phoned a guy I had only recently met (through

A New Life

a mutual friend) to ask if I could stay at his place. His apartment in Manhattan's Tribeca was my third move in three months. I stayed four months and the relationship was strictly platonic. I continued to spend every weekend at Bas'. He helped out financially and remained the one constant in my life. Though things seemed bleak, I still held on to the hope that some way, somehow, I would find a place of my own.

Lucky for me, a lady in the building I was living in was going away for the summer and needed to sublet her apartment. The rent was cheap, about four hundred a month, utilities included. "Borrowing" the money from Bas, I leaped at the opportunity, moving in the very day she left. The apartment was extremely junky and roach infested, but two weeks of cleaning and "Combat" took care of that. And it was well worth it. The two-bedroom apartment on the thirty-third floor had a terrace overlooking the Hudson River with a spectacular view of the Statue of Liberty.

At the end of the summer of 1986, the lady I sublet from returned to New York and I had to find another place immediately. When Bas phoned, I told him I had to move again. What he said next totally shocked me. "Constance, I'm really impressed by how you handled the tough times over the past year. You never complained or gave up, no matter how bad times got. You deserve a chance. Why don't you move into my place? Stay as long as you like." I wept silently. Finally I could feel some semblance of stability. Also, it was where I wanted to be.

GROUND CREW

*L*iving at Bas's offered some stability and a fresh start. I had lost practically everything, moving from place to place, and arrived at his doorstep with a mink coat, a diamond ring, a few pieces of clothing, and my sanity. Grateful for a place to stay and some desperately needed support, I went overboard, constantly cleaning and cooking elaborate down-home meals from scratch. It was what I had done in my relationship with Tony. Bas grabbed me gently by the shoulders one day and pleaded, "Relax! I don't need a twenty-course meal every day. I don't need you to do anything for me. Just concentrate on getting your life together. I told you, stay as long as you like. This is your home." It wasn't easy to relax when it had been over a year since I really had a home, and I didn't want to do anything to mess things up. Though certainly a challenge, life was gradually getting better. Over the next two months Bas and I began to bond, slowly becoming a family.

It had been some time since I had spoken with my real family. Transient the past year, I didn't want them to know how bad my situation was. Finally having a home and a phone I felt comfortable calling long distance on, I contacted them. I missed my sister Deb the most. It had been nearly three years since we last spoke.

We fell out of touch when, escaping a bad relationship, she moved from Cleveland to Portland, Oregon with her teenage daughters, Hope and Loreal. "Connie, I'm happier than I've ever been in my life!" Deb proclaimed victoriously. "I love the city, my home with Ras, who I've been with for two years now, and my work. I'm teaching African dance and have my own troupe called Black Minz. We're performing throughout Oregon and getting fantastic reviews." I was proud of my sister and extremely happy to be in contact again.

I had missed my mother as well. We began talking at least twice a week. Mom had moved back to South Carolina to care for her ninety-one-year-old mother whose health was beginning to fail. Her youngest son Mario and eldest sister Gertrude had also moved back. "I 'on really like it here," Mom admitted. "I miss Cleveland and all my friends, but what can I do? Mama need me."

I also contacted my brother Lester. Though our conversations were somewhat strained, he and I were enjoying our best relationship since early childhood. He was still married to his high school sweetheart and had a two-year-old daughter named Aiesha.

I tried to reestablish some kind of relationship with my sister Ernestine, who lived in Atlanta, Georgia with her husband and two daughters, Sonya and Keisha. Unreceptive, her conversations seemed forced and insincere. She rarely called me: I was usually the one who phoned. Ernestine rarely spoke to the other siblings either, and only called Mom occasionally. Eventually I took the hint and stopped calling altogether. Mom felt Ernestine had built up a barrier of resentment because she was left behind when my mother left Carlisle with the rest of her children. She eventually joined us in Cleveland at age eighteen, but I guess by then the damage had been done. My family had never been what one might call close. With us getting older, I wanted to try and change all that, but first I had to get *myself* together. I had reestablished some sort of foundation and was ready to rebuild my life. It was time to go to work.

I was ecstatic when Tracy phoned from Audrey Smaltz, Incorporated in the fall of 1986 with my first booking. Referred by my friend Kim, it had been over two long months since I initially inquired about work. When asked, "Are you available to dress two shows for Donna Karan?" I answered "Yes!" before Tracy could even complete the sentence. Karan was one of America's top designers and a personal favorite. The Spring 1987 collection was being shown at her 550 Seventh Avenue showroom, located in the heart of New York's bustling Garment District. I scribbled down the information.

"Dressers are required to wear a white top and black bottoms," said Tracy. "The pay is ten dollars an hour and paid in cash immediately following the show." There were to be twenty of us, one dresser for each model.

I was overly enthusiastic on the day of the show and arrived at Donna Karan's showroom a half-hour early. Surprisingly, a few dressers were already there. Easily recognizable in mandatory black and white, they gathered at a large-scale table in Karan's workroom for coffee and hors d'oeuvres, awaiting the arrival of their boss. "Audrey's real cool but she can be rough," warned middle-aged Brooklynite Yvonne Suggs, an opinion shared by a six-feet-tall black opera singer named Jennifer "Diva" Jones. Listening nearby, an affluently dressed and jeweled young lady named Theodora Kreatsoulas just smiled. They were from diverse cultural, ethnic, and economic backgrounds, but the dressers shared at least one thing in common: they loved the fashion biz. Dorthea Towles, the first black international model, worked for legendary fashion houses Dior, Balmain, and Balenciaga during the forties and fifties. Sydney Biddle Barrows, an attractive blonde in her thirties, was previously known as the infamous "Mayflower Madam."

Ground Crew

Listed on the social register, the Mayflower descendant became headline news when her call-girl operation, which catered to the rich and powerful, was busted. She authored a book about her experience, which was later made into a movie.

The dressers came to attention when a statuesque brown-skinned woman stormed into the workroom with her staff. Flawless in a black fitted designer dress; her head was wrapped in a long print scarf, which hung dramatically down her back. There was no doubt the striking figure was our boss, Audrey Smaltz. A dresser who walked in after her was quickly and sharply reprimanded. "You're late!" Audrey snapped as she carefully inspected the young lady from head to toe. "And weren't you told to wear black and white?" Audrey slowly turned away. "And pa—*leeze* don't let me see you in that *nasty* sweater again!" she beseeched. The young lady cowered under Audrey's loud harsh words. The other dressers turned away quickly.

I tried my best not to laugh as I carefully made my introductions to my employer and her staff: personal assistant Tracy, stage director BP Superstar, and makeup artist Al Grundy. I liked Audrey right off. Riotously funny with personality as big as her drag-queen-like gestures, she sounded her approval of me. "Alright girlfriend! You're working that sexy little outfit. [She was referring to my black leather-breasted top, leggings, and white shirt, borrowed from my friend Kim.] Now remember to check with Tracy to see who you're dressing," she said. "You have your pick of twenty models." In addition to providing the show's dressers and stage director, Audrey served as the model caller. Her job was to make sure each model was in line and ready to move when her turn came to walk down the runway.

The models started arriving, most of them recognizable from their numerous spreads in *Vogue* and *Harper's Bazaar*. A young Cindy Crawford arrived in jeans, no makeup, and disheveled hair.

Paulina Porizkova found a good spot to squat and read a paperback novel. Somalian-born beauty Iman walked into the room with the regality of a queen. Supermodels Christy Turlington and Linda Evangelista headed straight into the hair and makeup room for further enhancements by makeup artist Rex and master hairstylist Christaan. The remaining models—including Anna Bayle, Lisa Rutledge, Gail Elliott, Dalma, Diane Dewitt, Yasmeen Ghauri, Nell, Vanessa, Tara Shannon, and house model Doreen—ate, chatted, and sipped coffee or champagne as they waited their turns in the makeup and hair chairs.

The dressers were led from the workroom to the backstage area, already frenzied with activity. Donna Karan and her staff raced back and forth attending to last-minute details while fashion reporters and photographers scrambled for pictures and interviews. Each dresser was assigned a model and large garment rack filled with Karan's stunning creations. Beautiful suede and leather shoes stood at attention under each change of clothing. A clear plastic bag containing Robert Lee Morris accessories hung with each look. Dressers had to make a checklist of all items on, above, and below their assigned racks. Each outfit was numbered in the order in which it would be presented. To save precious time, all clothing was unbuttoned, unzipped, unsnapped, and untied prior to the show. Above the racks hung large white cards displaying the models' name and head shot. I was assigned to an exotic beauty named Dalma.

"All models in their first outfits!" Audrey bellowed, signaling the dressers into action. Everyone quickly retrieved their assigned model from the hair and makeup room, or wherever they were having their pre-show champagne. My model checked all her shoes for fit, then quickly unrobed down to her thong. After I speedily dressed her in a knockout navy crepe pantsuit, she did a quick once-over in a nearby mirror, then took her place in line. The

Ground Crew

models waited patiently for their cue as the designer and stylists make last-minute adjustments.

Seated and anxiously waiting, the audience was comprised primarily of the fashion media, buyers, celebrities, and socialites. People were seated according to their perceived importance, the front row being the most desirable spot. But no matter where they sat, Donna Karan was one of the hottest designers of the eighties and people were clamoring to get into her shows. The music started, casting a hush over the well-heeled audience and backstage.

"It's showtime!" shouted Audrey to the backstage crew. Tapping the show-opener's shoulder, she commanded, "Hit it, girlfriend!" and down the runway Doreen strutted, greeted by enthusiastic applause and a steady stream of flashing cameras. In no time at all it was my model's turn on the catwalk. Ever so serenely Dalma glided, occasionally executing the perfect spin, followed with a pose worthy of *Vogue*. After her stroll she raced backstage. Undoing her clothes as she ran, the veteran model was half disrobed by the time she reached our rack. I quickly finished undressing her, careful not to muss her sleek French twist. Her look secured, Dalma was off again. "I need Iman, Dalma, and Yasmeen—now!" shouted Audrey as she waved her clipboard frantically overhead. My model was already in line, and I hurriedly re-hung the previous look and prepared her next change. "I need Iman nowww!" Audrey yelled. "Who is Iman's dresser?"

I saw she was having some difficulty getting Iman ready in time, so I rushed to the overwhelmed dresser's aid. The African beauty had become irritated by the dresser's slowness and began dressing herself. "It's going to be a long show for this poor dresser," I thought. There were eight more super-quick changes to go and Iman wouldn't even let the girl touch her. Audrey shot a cold piercing stare at the panic-stricken dresser, who was certain to be dealt with later.

For the remainder of the show, I dressed my model as well as helping Iman's dresser. Never had I moved so fast. In less than half an hour it was all over. The audience and backstage crew applauded when all the models walked the runway for the big finale. They applauded even louder when the designer appeared. The elegant clothes, top models, great beauty staff, and best dressers on Seventh Avenue made the show a huge success. I was satisfied with the job I had done and apparently so was Audrey. "I like the way you pitched in and helped other dressers, Miss Connnstance," she said, popping her fingers. "Tracy will be calling you for more shows, girlfriend!"

Tracy called a month later for six more fashion shows, including Calvin Klein, Bern Conrad, and Adrienne Vittadini. Things happened quickly after that. Within four months, I was booked as assistant stylist for a Gucci show. A week later I helped to style and coordinate shows for Lane Bryant department store and furrier Adrian Landau, earning nearly a thousand dollars. It had been a while since I held that much money. "If only I could get paid steadily," I thought—"a check coming in every week."

Audrey's assistant Tracy confided in me that she was having difficulty working with her boss. Audrey's constant screaming and berating was making her a nervous wreck. Tracy wanted out, but needed to find a replacement so her boss wouldn't be inconvenienced. "Do you think Audrey would consider me for the position?" I asked.

"Wow! I think that's a great idea," said Tracy. "Audrey likes you and you can handle her temperament." On the few occasions Audrey yelled at me, I responded with laughter, causing her to laugh along and eventually calm down. "I'll have to clear everything with Audrey first but I'm sure there won't be a problem," Tracy assured me. She phoned the following day. "Congratulations. Audrey said yes." Finally, I had a steady job doing something I absolutely loved.

Doubling as Audrey's private residence, the midtown penthouse office was tastefully decorated with antiques, black memorabilia, and paintings by prominent black artists. The wall above my desk was covered with pictures of my boss with some of her famous acquaintances: Quincy Jones, Leontyne Price, then-vice president George Bush. I was extremely busy with my new full-time position at Audrey Smaltz, Incorporated, answering the high volume of calls, handling bookings, and serving as backstage supervisor at fashion shows. Working at Audrey's was never boring—and rarely quiet. Admittedly big, loud, and intimidating, Audrey constantly screamed and yelled because that was the way she knew to get results. Some of the dressers were scared of her. Hell, even some of the designers were afraid of her. She was highly respected in the fashion world and had been a beauty queen and model in her youth. "Born, bred, and buttered in Harlem, U.S.A.," the forty-nine-year-old fashion consultant became nationally known as commentator for the touring Ebony Fashion Fair shows and longtime girlfriend of jazz legend Lionel Hampton. Ten years earlier she founded the "Ground Crew," a backstage support group consisting of dressers, makeup artists, hairstylists, fashion stylists, show coordinators, and anyone else needed to get a fashion show off the ground. Audrey got the name Ground Crew from a Martin Luther King speech. She said, "It's the ground crew who gets the plane off the ground, darlin'."

I enjoyed working alongside Audrey at the office, but the best part of my job was working on all the fabulous shows. Though we worked throughout the year, New York Fashion Week was when most top designers showed their collections: Calvin Klein, Donna Karan, Issac Mizrahi, Escada, Arnold Scaasi, Rebecca Moses, Carmelo Pomodoro, Carolyne Roehm. It was a thrill meeting the iconoclastic Halston while working on Bill Dugan's show. It was also exciting meeting Christian Lacroix. His show at the Winter

Garden was the most spectacular I had ever seen. Opulence and glitz were in vogue during the late eighties and fashion's new star, Parisian designer Lacroix, was the master. His first showing in the States drew the top names in fashion, entertainment, and society. The press was out in great numbers as well. Reporter Teri Agins was there to do a story on the Ground Crew for the *Wall Street Journal*. We made the front page.

The Ground Crew got recognition usually not given a backstage crew. Audrey produced two fashion shows for the *Oprah Winfrey* show. Two other television shows, *48 Hours* and *CBS This Morning* did segments on us. It was amazing to see myself in action backstage on national television. A two-page story on us dressing the Adrienne Vittadini show appeared in the fashion section of the *Florida Times-Union*. Entitled "Ground Crew Get the Show on the Runway," the article featured a large color picture of Adrienne, Audrey, and me looking over a rack of the designer's creations. When my picture appeared in *Harper's Bazaar*, my sister Ernestine who rarely called, phoned from her home in Georgia. "I was at the beauty salon leafing through *Bazaar* and was shocked when I saw your picture!" she said excitedly. "I screamed to everyone in the salon, 'That's my sister! That's my sister!'" Getting press was fantastic but to gain some semblance of financial independence, I needed at least one good payday. The Ground Crew was booked to do a show that would do just that.

Audrey landed a big government contract to produce a fashion show for the Harlem Urban Development Corporation, headed by the handsome and distinguished Donald Cogsville. We met with Mr. Cogsville and his assistant at the Harlem State Office Building almost daily working out the details. The government had plans to build a major development along the Hudson River at 125th Street. A fashion show was the event selected to publicly

Ground Crew

announce the ambitious plans. Audrey was given full license to produce the show, along with a whopping budget.

The event was christened "Harlem on the Hudson" and subtitled "Honey, We're Having a Fierce Fashion Show!" We worked ten to twelve hours daily preparing for the big show. "It's going to be an international third-world fashion extravaganza!" Audrey proclaimed. Designers from Bukino Faso, the West Indies, Paris, and New York would be represented. Among the New York designers were Betsy Gonsales, Fabrice, Lester Hyatt, and black furrier James McQuay. Celebrated designer Patrick Kelly was also being represented in the show.

Born black and poor in Vicksburg, Mississippi, Patrick Kelly rose to prominence in the Parisian fashion world with designs and accessories that were creative, modern, and fun. Some had a "black memorabilia" edge: watermelon hats, "jigaboo" purses, little black baby-doll pins. Patrick became best known for his creative use of buttons, used by the hundreds on many of his designs. His fashion shows were anticipated events, original and exciting from start to finish. Audrey flew to Paris every season to work on the shows, which featured innovative designs and some of the best black walkers in modeling.

In-house makeup artist and second in command at Audrey Smaltz, Incorporated, Al Grundy was in charge of selecting the long list of models for "Harlem on the Hudson." It included former Vogue cover girl Peggy Dillard, Toukie Smith, Bo Pinder, Sharon "Magic" Jordan, Jerushia MacDonald, Suzy MacDonald, Delores Henderson, Charissa Craig, Coco, Olivia Chapman, Rosalind Johnson, Princess Shola, David Martin, Rudi Hamilton, and Renauld White.

I was booked as a stylist for the show, as were aspiring Brooklyn designer Mad Scott and a Ground Crew newcomer named Barbara Bennett. Light brown-skinned and attractive, with big hair and an even bigger smile, she said she had been a model in Australia. She was best known for being singer Roberta Flack's stylist and for hobnobbing with the rich and famous. Another stylist was brought in at the last minute, twenty-two-year-old Jerome "Jo" Reid, a West Indian and Danish pretty-boy with long dark hair and a sexy accent. He was also an aspiring designer who had just arrived from Paris where he worked with Audrey on a Patrick Kelly show. With all the clothes, models, beauty staff, and stylists, Audrey's penthouse office became a showroom and makeshift runway as we prepared for the big production.

Scheduled for a beautiful warm September day, the show was held outside, using the Hudson River and clear blue sky as backdrops. A giant white tent had been constructed to house the backstage and the T-shaped runway was the largest I had ever seen. Backstage was chaotic but exhilarating, packed with the top names in black beauty and fashion. The dressers readied their full racks of clothing. Models lined up for makeup and hair with a team of wizards headed by Al Grundy and James Harris. The music and sound people checked and rechecked their equipment. Our styling team checked accessories and made last-minute clothing adjustments.

The show had an even bigger turnout than expected. Hundreds of seats were quickly filled, with just as many people standing. The atmosphere was electric with excitement and anticipation. Looking stunning in a short, low-cut red dress and clutching a mike, Audrey sashayed onto the runway and loudly pronounced, "It's an international third-world fashion show for the *first* time ever *here* in Harlem, and it was *fa-ree* to all of you! *How* about that!" Michael Jackson's hit "Bad" blasted out and the first model hit the runway in a Betsy Gonsales original. Audrey's commentary was fast-paced and entertaining, filled with sass and humor. "Betsy says don't take a taxi. Wear this and stop traffic. Flaunt your *ass*-sets!"

Ground Crew

All the models were good but the plus-size girls took the show. When one big and beautiful green-eyed model appeared, Audrey yelled playfully, "What did yo mama feed you, darlin'?" The audience applauded. "I can tell you what," said Audrey. "She fed her well!" They cheered even louder. When curvaceous Toukie Smith walked down the runway in a skintight animal-print number that showcased her large boobs, tiny waist, and high round "tuckas," the audience went wild. Over the thunderous applause, Audrey shouted, "Some folk say it's what's *up front* that counts; and then some people say it's what's *following you* that counts. Baaaby, Miss Toukie got it *coming-and-going*!" That said, Toukie struck a pose, then turned and headed up the runway, slowly and sensuously switching her voluptuous backside. "Alright, Mama! Y'all hittin' it today!" Audrey yelled. The audience loved it!

Audrey was exuberant from start to finish! At one point she stopped midsentence to announce the arrival of long-time beau, Lionel Hampton. "Daddy Gates? Is that you over there? Ahhh my baby's here," she beamed. Running a little over an hour, the show was the longest I had ever worked on, but every minute was packed with surprise and excitement. The backstage crew did an excellent job: inspired by the audience, models, and especially Audrey, who ended the show with a speech. "Be loyal to yourself, to your hair, to your lips, to your skin, to your Southern-smile-and-laughter. Farewell, my deep and Africanic brothers. Be brave, keep freedom in the family, and *do-what-you-can-for-the-white-folks*!" At that point she broke out in dance followed by the show's entire staff, tossing confetti I had cut up at the last minute. The crowd roared!

After the Harlem show, work starting pouring in so Audrey hired Jerome "Jo" Reid (stylist on Harlem show) to help out in the office. Worldly and extremely talented, I enjoyed his company. After working together all day we often hung out in the

Village or at his Chelsea apartment planning our futures in fashion. Jo made me feel special. He respected my business acumen and, even though my wardrobe was sparse at the time, made me feel like the epitome of high fashion. "Fashion is more about attitude and personal style than anything," he said, "and you have both. But Miss Constance, a diva has to at least have the basics. Girlfriend, I'm taking you shopping." A gifted designer, he also promised to make four knockout dresses for me, free of charge.

To one of the most thoughtful and generous things any friend had ever done for me, I said, "Thank you."

A smart-mouthed Jo replied, "Well, everyone knows the best way to get along with Miss Constance is to kiss her ass." I pretended not to hear. "Besides," he said, "you need fierce pieces for fashion parties, and I need my work to be seen by the right people."

As an employee of ASI, sometimes I had to attend industry parties. "Night of Stars" was a celebration being held at The Waldorf-Astoria to honor the world's fashion elite. Audrey informed me I would be attending, along with her and two other ladies from the Ground Crew. "Patrick Kelly's flying in from Paris for the event and you girls are going to be part of his entourage," she said.

"Really? Fabulous!" I replied.

"Yeahhhh! Patrick's girls!" Audrey yelled with a snap of her fingers.

Required to wear current Patrick Kelly designs to the event, a trip to Warnaco, the New York-based company in charge of the designer's line, would be necessary. We would borrow whatever was needed from rooms of fabulously fun PK clothes and accessories. Jo pulled me aside to volunteer his services as my stylist. "No glitz! A simple black dress with a fierce neckline is all you'll need, girlfriend," he assured me in his thick Danish accent. "I'll do the rest." A black stretch-velvet knee-length dress with a scooped neckline was my choice. A clear hard-plastic envelope filled with

Ground Crew

different colored satin bows came with the dress. The idea was to pin the bows onto the dress. Jo had other plans.

Armed with a shopping bag full of outrageous feathers, Jo arrived at my place early on the day of the affair to style my wardrobe as well as my hair. "Okay, girlfriend, let's get ready to get fierce!" he said. "First, your hair." Atop my head, he wrapped my long ponytail into a neat twist. Then he placed a black ostrich plume in the center and two peacock feathers on each side. The effect was dramatic, very Josephine Baker.

"Fabulous!" I whispered.

"Now get dressed!" Jo ordered. His hands full with feathers, he swooned when I came out of the bathroom in the sexy black dress. "Turn around girlfriend!" he said as he stepped back for a better view. "Wait! I got it!" he shouted. "I know exactly what that dress needs!" Just above the derriere Jo attached a black ostrich plume, highlighted with two peacock feathers. "Now for your purse," he pondered, examining the clear plastic envelope that came with the dress. "I know, let's really gag the kids!" He removed the satin bows from inside the envelope and pinned them on the outside. My look was finished with black satin pumps, a luxurious blanket-sized cashmere wrap, and a few dabs of Coco by Chanel.

"How do I look?" I asked.

"Girlfriend, they-are-going-to-*hate*-you!" Jo gleamed triumphantly. "Promise you'll call first thing tomorrow with all the dish. I'm especially interested in Patrick's reaction to what I did with his dress." Jo had previously worked with the designer but left under unfavorable circumstances. I never dared to ask what they were. After looking me over one last time, Jo escorted me downstairs to hail a taxi—and to help maneuver my bustle and headdress into the back seat. I rode the entire way on my side with my headdress hanging out the window.

She Can Go Where Pretty Girls Go

"Night of Stars" was a spectacular, glamorous event. Limousines lined The Waldorf-Astoria while the exquisitely dressed made their way inside. After having a cocktail in the hotel lounge, I ran into Patrick Kelly and several of his "girls" in the lobby. The bearded designer was dressed in his signature denim overalls to which he creatively added black-tie accessories. After greeting me with fashion's customary kiss on both cheeks and a big smile, he commented, "I really love what you've done with my dress and bows."

"Thanks," I said, smiling back.

"Come join us," he said. "We're on our way up." I joined his entourage as we headed upstairs for the party.

We piled into the already crowded elevator. On the ride up my feathered headdress lodged itself in the face of a lady who held the unfortunate position directly behind me. I tried moving my head, but space being limited, matters were only made worse. The poor woman complained as she tried unsuccessfully to remove my plumes from her face. I really felt badly for her and a little embarrassed for myself, but it took everything I had to keep from laughing. When we got off the elevator (thankfully the ride was short), I turned to apologize. To my surprise the lady was Bianca Jagger, seventies fashion plate and ex-wife of rock legend, Mick Jagger. She forced a faint smile, accepted my apology, and quickly distanced herself from my feathers *and* me.

The grand ballroom was filled with the crème de la crème of international fashion. I spotted Audrey at the bar, looking remarkable in a Patrick Kelly leopard print dress and upswept hairdo. "Miss *Connn*stance, you look *beyond* fabulous!" she said. "And yo little titties looking right cute in that dress, girlfriend!" I blushed. After another quick glance and sip from her champagne glass, Audrey snapped her fingers. "Work it, Miss *Connn*stance!"

I was even more flattered when asked, along with two other ladies, to hand out awards to designers being honored that night.

Ground Crew

All smile and feathers, I walked to the podium to present an award to Italian superstar Gianni Versace. He smiled approvingly at my dress and kissed both sides of my face before giving an enthusiastically received acceptance speech. It was the highlight of a very special evening.

When Jo came by the following day, I told him about my evening and of Patrick's positive reaction to his styling. But he seemed preoccupied. "What's wrong?" I asked.

"I'm worried about my job with Audrey," he said solemnly. "You know she doesn't like me very much, Miss Constance. Remember when, in front of a room full of people she actually said, 'Jo? Patrick said the reason he fired you was because you acted like a big faggot!'"

"Yeah, I remember," I said. "And I also remember your nonchalant response: 'He was just upset because he wanted me but could not have me.'" Jo always had great comebacks for Audrey's assaults. But with her becoming more hostile toward him, he felt his days with the Ground Crew were numbered. And he was right. Audrey let him go a month later. With no other means of support, he moved back to Denmark shortly afterwards. A dear friend and major source of inspiration, I missed him terribly.

Another big inspiration from the Ground Crew was a remarkable twenty-two-year-old Puerto Rican named Alvaro, an extraordinary artist whose work captured the very souls of his subjects. Spirited and handsome with long black hair, broad shoulders, and a billion-dollar personality, he also captured the fashion world's heart. Alvaro had come a long way since his early days as protégé to famous illustrator Antonio Lopez and was quickly gaining a reputation as one of fashion's most talented artists. He met the supermodels backstage while dressing shows, forming friendships with the likes of Iman, Naomi Campbell, and others. From those associations came more lucrative bookings and higher visibility. As Alvaro's star rose he dressed fewer shows and gave more parties to promote his many projects, including a calendar for the Elite Modeling Agency featuring a supermodel for every month of the year.

Alvaro and I became close friends, supporters of one another's work. I supported him by attending most of his promo parties. As dressers' supervisor, I also made him supervisor at the fashion shows, giving him easier access to the models. He was a monumental help to me as well. Whenever I needed fresh faces for the Ground Crew, I called on Alvaro, an unlimited resource of aspiring young talent, eager to work. Alvaro made me feel beautiful as well. Growing up, I had always felt my thick lips were unattractive. "Uh uhhh, Miss Constance, are you kidding? Your mouth is genuis!" he responded whenever I made negative comments about my lips. In fact he did dozens of sketches of me, on occasion drawing my lips onto the sexy women he was becoming famous for painting. Always a positive energy source, there was never a down moment with Alvaro. "Miss Constance, you wanna laugh?" was how he began when he phoned. When we got together, it was worse: we laughed at any and everything—except for the speed at which his career was going. Eventually he became so successful he stopped dressing shows altogether. There were major ad campaigns for designers and stores, magazine covers, television appearances, and constant mentions in the gossip columns for his outrageous antics, which sometimes included fighting. Even after Alvaro stopped dressing shows, he remained my most important resource for talent as well as friend and advisor.

Like Alvaro, by the fall of 1988 I was working nonstop but unlike him, I still wasn't making enough money. Audrey loaned me out to Gotfried and Loving, a public relations firm, two days a week to assist with a campaign for Hanes hoisery. The experience was valuable but did little to help my finances. Although

Ground Crew

working with other dressing crews was forbidden, I took outside jobs, working with designers like John Anthony and Karl Lagerfeld for Chanel. Another source of income came from showroom and department store display work. I did everything from decorating Christmas trees for Lord and Taylor to assisting with costumes for the Macy's Thanksgiving Day Parade. All that and I still didn't have much money.

After long and careful consideration I decided to stop working with the Ground Crew. When I told Alvaro I was thinking of going into business for myself, he shouted, "Go for it! Bring it!" It was difficult telling Audrey, whom I adored, respected, and had learned so much from, that I was quitting.

"Miss *Connn*stance, you can't go!" she said. "I need you here." Then she generously offered a small percentage of each show. As an added inducement, she allowed me to work from home four days out of the week, although I'd have to phone in daily and continue to supervise the dressers. I agreed to her offer even though quitting would have been preferable. Starting my own company and working for Audrey would definitely be a conflict of interest. "At least I'll be getting a raise and it'll be convenient booking shows from home," I rationalized.

After awhile, working with the Ground Crew became absolute torture. Following a Donna Karan show I told Audrey I was quitting. "I love you dearly, but I have to pursue my own interests," I added. We parted with the understanding that I would do three more shows, already booked.

But when Audrey heard rumors that I was starting my own business she said solemnly, "Constance, I won't be needing you any longer." She was hurt and a little bitter for awhile but I understood. I would miss her too.

She Can Go Where Pretty Girls Go

In New York City, Bas and me on New Years Eve, 1989.

With best friend Kim (at right).

Ground Crew

Ground Crew in Harper's Bazaar, 1989. Audrey Smaltz and me (center, facing).

She Can Go Where Pretty Girls Go

Me backstage at Donna Karan fashion show. Model Iman in background.

Backstage at Donna Karan. A young Cindy Crawford with Ground Crew dressers.

Ground Crew
———————

Backstage at Spy Magazine fashion show. Actress comedienne Sandra Bernhart at right, me in center.

She Can Go Where Pretty Girls Go

On a break from work at Audrey Smaltz, Inc.

STYLE ARCHITECT

$\mathcal{I}$ was determined to start my own business. Acting on a tip that the American Cancer Society was looking for someone to produce a benefit fashion show, I secured a meeting with an executive from the organization. We met for lunch at Windows on the World, atop the World Trade Center's Twin Towers. My presentation was good but apparently not good enough to land the account. Undaunted, I remained open for the next opportunity. I needed just one good client to make a name for myself, along with a super talented staff.

Stylist Barbara Bennett was producing a benefit fashion show for Harlem's Abyssinian Baptist Church and asked if I'd supervise the backstage. Having worked together on countless shows, she commented, "because nobody works a backstage like Miss Constance!" I rode with the stylist-turned-producer on show day to help transport clothing. "Reverend Calvin Butts is participating as well as the actor Taimak," said Barbara excitedly as she jockeyed for a parking space near the church entrance. Waiting just outside the church door was a husky, ruggedly attractive brown-skinned man with cloudy green eyes, a short widow-peaked curl, and a big grin. "You know Quietfire, don't you Miss Constance?" asked

Barbara. "He's going to be doing the make up." It was our first meeting in person, but I had spoken with him several times when he phoned Audrey's office to speak with her or Al.

Super-talented, quick-witted, and hyper-driven—although hired to do makeup, Quietfire also helped backstage, organizing clothing and getting the models dressed. I liked him. After Barbara's show (a big success), we got a chance to talk further. Since he lived at 106th and Manhattan Avenue, not far from my place at 96th and Amsterdam, we took the subway together. Quietfire hated being called by his real name, Ronald Easter, and swore to anyone who doubted the authenticity of his moniker, "I'm half Cherokee!" The thirty-seven-year-old New York native had been a celebrity of sorts. There was some success as a model and later as a modeling agent. Bigger success came as makeup artist to the stars, his most notable client being pop diva Whitney Houston. He had worked with the singer almost from the start of her career and had established a close relationship. Quietfire was estranged from his star client for the past year, had fallen on hard times, and was on the verge of losing his apartment. He admitted that drug use and a lack of managerial skills led to the demise of his once-lucrative career. Though sympathetic about his current situation, I was impressed—and then flattered when he asked me, "Would you like to model?"

"Model? No!" I answered, chuckling at the thought of my thirty-five-year-old butt sashaying down a runway.

"Then what do you want to do?" he asked.

"Well, I would like my own agency."

"For dressers?"

"Well, yeah, but mostly for make up artists, hair stylists, and fashion stylists."

"Really?" He half grinned and raised one eyebrow. "Well then, why don't you do it? I tell you what. You can be *my* agent."

"Are you serious?"

"Quite! I've heard great things about you and I like how you handled yourself at Audrey's. And look at how well we just worked together on Barbara's show." It didn't take much convincing.

"I'd love to rep you!" I said, a million ideas jetting through my head. The teaming was perfection. I knew the fashion industry and he knew the music business. We planned to take both by storm

Armed with a list of fashion show personnel, one extremely talented makeup artist, supportive friends and boyfriend, I was ready for business. "We'll be image-makers for the record industry and backstage support for the fashion business," I told my best friend Kim, who generously offered her support. She was doing okay financially, working in cosmetics at the Chanel boutique and living on Sixty-fifth in Madison.

"Do you need to borrow some money for start-up capital?" she offered.

"No, but thanks," I answered.

"Well, if you need anything, just let me know."

What I needed was a good strong name for my company. I called on my friend since childhood, Jackie Carson, for help. After three years of silence over something "he said, she said," we were speaking again. She had given up her lingerie shop and was working at Saks Fifth Avenue in cosmetics. Initially I asked her to go into business with me but she refused. "I want to do my own thing," she said. "Maybe work with plastic surgeons doing makeovers for their patients." After three days of tossing around every combination we could think of, we came up with the perfect name for my company.

The doors of "Style Architect" opened on November 18, 1988, from the Upper-West-Side studio I shared with my boyfriend, Bas. I couldn't have done it without him. After working all day at *his* job, he came home and helped *me*. We decorated an area to serve as my office. Bas purchased office equipment and gave me five hundred dollars to start a business account as well as money for promotions. Printed by the hundreds, advertisements were mailed to every record company, fashion design house, magazine, public relations firm, photographer, and ad agency in town. Appointments were made to show Quietfire's slightly dated but still impressive portfolio.

Gradually bookings started coming in. An album cover for singer Will Downing paid well. A cover for jazz musician Stanley Jordan didn't. Some bookings paid little or nothing, but we took them in hopes of being brought in on lucrative jobs later. One such booking came from a director who had recently started a Hispanic production company. She wanted Quietfire to do make up for a televised public service announcement with award-winning actors Morgan Freeman and Rita Moreno. We met with the young female director at Golden Globe winner Morgan Freeman's West End apartment to work out details. It didn't take long to agree on a rate. The budget was so low there was little room for negotiation. Unenthusiastic about the job, Quietfire asked me, "Please go to the booking with me, Mommie."

He didn't get off to a good start with Tony, Emmy, Grammy, and Academy Award winner Rita Moreno. When Quietfire tried to apply the actress's foundation using a shade he felt suitable for her coloring, she recoiled. "Oh no, that's too dark!"

"The color's perfect for you," he assured her. Unconvinced, Moreno refused to let him apply it. She refused to even speak to him directly. Instead, she directed her conversation toward me. When the frustrated makeup artist left the room for a "breather," the actress walked over to the makeup box and chose a much lighter foundation. Upon Quietfire's return, she announced that she had found her true color. He thought the makeup was far

Style Architect

too light but obliged her and did an excellent job making it look natural. Miss Moreno seemed pleased with the results, but still continued to direct all conversation to me. After the multitalented Moreno left the room, Quietfire swiped, "She knows that makeup is too light for her, but she just had to have a lily-white-woman beat." Morgan Freeman was a much easier subject for Quietfire. The actor was calm and pleasant, and it only took fifteen minutes to do his grooming. Displeased with the booking on the whole, Quietfire was ready to leave. When the director asked, "Stay, just in case Miss Moreno needs retouching," he quipped, "My makeup don't move!" left her some face powder in a paper towel, then dashed. Nothing more ever came from that booking. And Style Architect still didn't have *one* regular client.

At least twice a week Quietfire and I made the rounds, visiting A&R personnel at the top record labels. We offered them a discounted rate to work with new artists. If they hit big, we would be used for all their bookings at our regular rate. Mary Moore, who worked in Artist Development at Arista, readily agreed to our terms. "I have absolutely no budget," she warned. She needed make up for an Arista group comprised of four pretty petite sisters named the Braxtons. Booked for the group's live performance at a midtown club, I went with Quietfire to support and assist. The show was excellent: Those sisters could really sing, especially the sultry-voiced lead, Toni. The Braxtons, however, didn't fare well as a group and were dropped from the label. Lead singer Toni Braxton went solo, signed with LaFace Records, and the rest is pop history. We only worked with her twice after she "blew up."

Even though Toni Braxton didn't become a regular client, we were still working regularly. BET's (Black Entertainment Television) Lydia Cole engaged Quietfire to do several artists' makeup for a listening party at the Meridian Hotel, including Bobbi

She Can Go Where Pretty Girls Go

Humphrey, Eric Gale, and an unknown girl group named En Vogue. A quartet, Cynthia was sweet; Dawn, sexy; Terry, a beauty; and Max, stylish, friendly, and the most outgoing. "Gimme those boots!" she demanded playfully, her eyes fixed on my treasured black suede Roger Viviers. At the listening party, attended by nearly a hundred industry heavies, all the acts were good but En Vogue was phenomenal! Their voices, beauty, and tremendous sex appeal left little doubt they were headed for superstardom. Unfortunately, they only used our services twice after the BET listening party but Quietfire and I remained optimistic.

Exciting and more financially rewarding opportunities came from Island Records, revamping the image of R&B trio By All Means and creating one for hip-hop ingenue Tam Tam. Quietfire did makeup, I assisted with styling, and we brought in a hair stylist from Baltimore, Maryland, named Keith Hayes. Though we were paid well, neither act went anywhere. When we got our first major video (We Can Spend the Night) with popular recording artists Guy, it looked as if things were starting to pick up, but there was only one more project with them.

Style Architect's first regular client came in the form of Toukie Smith, a voluptuous black bombshell with blonde hair, high cheekbones, and an overbite that gave an interesting edge to her unique beauty. Energetic and very vocal, Toukie often punctuated her sentences with loud finger snaps. I initially met her while working for Audrey Smaltz. She was a former model and sister of celebrated late designer Willi Smith. She also became well known as longtime girlfriend of movie star Robert DeNiro. Coming into her own, Toukie had started her own company, Hot Box, Inc., and booked her beauty team through Style Architect. There were photo shoots with *French Vogue, German Elle,* and *Interview* magazines and television appearances on Joan Lunden and David Letterman. Her big break came when she landed a role on the television

Style Architect

sitcom, *227*. Adding to an already busy schedule, Toukie was promoting a benefit in honor of her late brother.

"Willi Smith Day" was to be a star-studded benefit to raise money to fight AIDS, which had claimed so many lives, including that of the famous designer. The much-publicized event was to be held at Robert DeNiro's new downtown restaurant, Tribeca Grill. Toukie worked tirelessly promoting the benefit. She booked Quietfire for a promotional appearance a day prior to the big event. Amazingly, he stood her up. I was outraged! So was Toukie when she phoned. "Come on now girlfriend, this is business! I'm about professionalism—okaaay? Just to let you know, I will *not* be using Quiet again!"

After apologizing profusely, I said, "I'll get you a fabulous replacement immediately and I promise this will never happen again."

"Let's go to the next level, girlfriend!" she insisted.

Having drawn from the artist's well of resources in the past, I called Alvaro as soon as I hung up from Toukie. "Hello darling, I'm in a spot."

"What's wrong, Miss Constance?"

"Do you know of a super fabulous make up artist who could do Toukie's make up, like *now*? Quietfire stood us up."

"Byron Barnes!" Alvaro answered quickly. "I think he's better than Quiet." Luckily, Byron graciously stepped in, saving my reputation and client. When Toukie phoned that evening her tone was entirely different.

"Girlfriend, that Byron is fabulous! I want to book him for Willi Smith Day." She invited me as well.

The night before the benefit, I visited Barbara Bennett at her cozy Central Park West apartment. Toukie had chosen the stylist to supervise the backstage for a celebrity fashion show being presented at the gala. As Barbara filled me in on the latest overwhelming problem she was facing as supervisor, the phone rang.

She Can Go Where Pretty Girls Go

"Excuse me Miss Constance, let me get that. Hello? It's Quietfire for you," said Barbara. I knew it was going to be unpleasant.

As soon as I spoke, in his nastiest and most intimidating voice, Quietfire yelled, "Don't get it twisted, sistuh! Even if I miss a booking, you are *never* to replace me! Fuck what you heard! You're never to rep any other makeup artist but *me*!" He was so loud Barbara reacted from a few feet away. I was boiling mad!

"This is my damn company Quietfire, and I'll rep whomever I please!" I yelled, then slammed down the receiver.

"Don't get upset, Miss Constance," said Barbara. "You know how Quietfire is. You took care of your client Miss Toukie and that's all that matters."

Invited to Toukie's benefit as well, Alvaro and I shared a taxi to Tribeca Grill on the day of the big event, joking and laughing the entire ride. When we arrived photographers were snapping pictures of everyone entering the restaurant; including us. We had to push pass them and a crowd of onlookers to get inside. Doing his best Marilyn Monroe impression, Alvaro quipped, "That was simply elegant." I laughed. "No, really!" he said, still in character. Barbara Bennett was the first familiar face we spotted. She introduced me to Bethann Hardison, head of one of the city's top modeling agencies and her son, actor Kadeem Hardison, star of the hit sitcom, *A Different World*. The restaurant served up a banquet of celebrities: Robert DeNiro, Christopher Walden, Quincy Jones, Martin Scorcese, Gregory Hines, Harvey Keitel, Cicely Tyson, and the first black mayor of New York City, David Dinkins.

After speaking to a few familiar faces, including my old boss, Audrey Smaltz, Alvaro and I went upstairs where the fashion show was to be held. We checked in on Toukie and my new makeup artist before going backstage. The very first person we saw was Quietfire, who had been enlisted as one of the celebrity models. "You slammin' like a door on a Lincoln in that Donna Karan suede

Style Architect

suit!" he smiled. After removing a stray hair from my eye he said, "You know I'm sorry, Mommie." Then he kissed me on both cheeks. Naturally I forgave him. As well as liking him, he was a very important component of Style Architect. I just wanted him to understand that nothing less than professionalism would be tolerated.

With Quietfire's and my relationship somewhat restored, Alvaro suggested, "Let's get a sip." We found a waiter, some champagne, and ringside seats for the fashion show. I had a fantastic time and met some fascinating people. Some would become future clients.

Quietfire and I worked diligently trying to get Whitney Houston as a client. We phoned her company, Nippy, Inc., regularly. Administrative assistant Maria Padulla was fabulous, usually putting us straight through to whomever we wanted. We spoke two-way with Whitney's sister-in-law Donna Houston, who patiently listened to our constant pitches for work. "Y'all don't love me no more," said Quietfire. She assured him they did. Whitney's dad John Houston was in charge and sometimes took time from his busy schedule to speak. Her manager Robyn Crawford usually tried to avoid us. When we did reach her, she was brief.

Relentless, we went to Nippy Inc.'s Englewood Cliffs, New Jersey, office unannounced, usually winding up in Donna's office because she was the only one who'd put up with us for any length of time. "What y'all got coming up? When y'all gonna book me?" asked Quietfire. Constantly reminding Donna of his availability, he clearly missed working with Whitney and her staff. He adored the singer and also missed the money and perks that came with being on the inside.

Finally, In June of 1989 came the call we had been waiting for. Whitney's office booked Quietfire to do the singer's makeup for a special issue of *Rolling Stone* magazine. He would be working with mom Cissy Houston as well. "Thank you, Jesus!" shouted Quietfire when I phoned with news of the booking. "Please let it be a cover!" When "The Rock and Roll Photo Album" issue of *Rolling Stone* hit the newsstands in September: instead of the cover we hoped for, Whitney and her mom appeared in a small picture inside. Quietfire was a little disappointed. "That picture's no larger than a postage stamp!" he complained. It *was* a little small but Whitney and Cissy looked absolutely fabulous! So did my company's name appearing in the credits. Things were starting to look up. Quietfire was back in the extremely exclusive Nippy, Inc. camp and Style Architect finally had its superstar client.

We heard through the grapevine that Whitney was having a huge party to celebrate her twenty-sixth birthday. I phoned for invites. Two poster-sized invitations arrived picturing Houston in a sexy black dress. They read: "You are cordially invited to attend an outdoor barbecue in celebration of Whitney Houston's twenty-sixth birthday, August 12, from 4:00–12:00 p.m. [sic]. Dinner served at 8:30. Dress summer vogue. Tennis and swimming available."

"What would I wear to a barbecue and what is summer vogue?" I wondered. I wasn't worried though. Having an agency made borrowing clothes from designers easy. After pulling four looks from two showrooms, I settled on a black Patrick Kelly bustier jumpsuit with matching jacket.

It rained lightly on the day of Whitney's big party. Dressed in all black and looking pulled-together himself, Quietfire did a beautiful job on my makeup and cut and reworked my short dated curls into a stylish straight do. We arrived at Houston's Mendham, New Jersey, estate in an embarrassing old town car driven by a friend of my boyfriend's, owner of a small car service in the Bronx. It was the best we could do. The limousine services in Manhattan wanted a small fortune to drive the long distance. Still, I was embarrassed when the valet tried to open my door and the handle broke off. Quietfire leaned over and shook the door a few times before it finally opened.

Style Architect

There was a long receiving line going into the party. Whitney was personally greeting her guests, along with mother Cissy, the first person Quietfire introduced me to. She looked me over carefully before shaking my hand. Then I met Whitney for the very first time. "This is my agent, Constance," Quietfire beamed, as he introduced us. He had told her about me earlier at the *Rolling Stone* shoot. Wearing sparse, clean makeup and her shoulder-length hair in soft curls, she looked younger and more beautiful in person. I smiled as we shook hands, wished her a happy birthday, then handed her a beautifully wrapped box containing an oversized bottle of Chanel No. 5 perfume.

"Thank you, Miss Constance," she smiled, motioning a man standing beside her to take the gift. Then the singer and Quietfire spoke privately for a moment while I headed for the bar to calm my nerves after the long uncomfortable ride. Shortly afterwards, Quietfire joined me. "She called you Miss Constance!" he grinned. "She likes you! I can tell." That was great to hear. I was certainly impressed by her.

Houston's sprawling estate was also very impressive. A palatial, contemporary white mansion dominated the entrance. A few yards away stood the pool house and fully equipped outdoor bar. Since it had been raining on and off since morning, Whitney had the vast, manicured grounds covered with giant magnificent white tents. Long narrow tents connected them so you could walk from one to the next with out getting your designer duds wet.

There were many designer outfits at the party—on some of the world's most recognizable faces: singer Natalie Cole, Arista Record's Clive Davis, movie star Eddie Murphy, gospel singer Bebe Winans. After getting champagne Quietfire and I ran into singer Freddy Jackson in the dance tent. "Walk, girl!" he hollered, before imitating my walk to show he too could strut. We laughed, then turned our attention to the party heating up on the dance floor.

She Can Go Where Pretty Girls Go

New York newscaster Rolanda Watts was wearing a short tight number and dancing dirty and lowdown. Singer-turned-psychic-hotline entrepreneur Dionne Warwick danced balancing a half-full wineglass in her hand. Whitney took the floor with partner, ex–New Edition member-turned-hot-solo-artist Bobby Brown. She looked sophisticated in a tailored white pantsuit. He looked like a little boy in his Gumby-style haircut and matching baggy top and shorts. None of us knew it at the time but the dance partners, who at that time were mere acquaintances, would one day become one of the most talked about unions in show biz history.

After dancing a couple times ourselves, Quietfire and I walked to another tent for something to eat. We helped ourselves to the buffet then sat at a beautifully set table with Whitney's choreographer, Khandi Alexander. Before Quietfire could introduce us, she whispered to him, "Who is she?"

"My agent, Constance," he replied.

Dissatisfied with his answer, she asked me directly, "You're a model?"

"No, I really am Quietfire's agent," I answered.

"Ummm huh. Actress?" she asked. I don't know if we ever convinced Khandi of my profession, but we all had a fun time chatting throughout dinner.

Far too soon for me, the party started winding down around midnight. Before leaving, Quietfire and I spoke briefly with Whitney and said our farewells to Robyn Crawford, a very pregnant Donna Houston, and record producer Narada Michael Walden. It was the most fabulous party I had ever gone to and I met some extraordinary people, most notably, Whitney. She was the biggest star in the world, yet one of the least pretentious people I had ever met.

After Whitney Houston became a client, Style Architect grew faster than I ever could have imagined. We worked nonstop with

166

Style Architect

Whitney for publicity work, magazine shoots, commercials, personal appearances, videos, concert dates, and televised awards shows: the *Academy Awards, Grammy Awards, American Music Awards, Billboard Awards, Soul Train Awards,* and the *NAACP Image Awards.* Finally, Style Architect was an agency to be reckoned with.

I was amazed at all the attention I was receiving because of my agency's association with Houston. Whenever she appeared on television, it seemed like everyone I knew would call. And *People* magazine phoned twice trying to get information. I was also invited to go on the *Geraldo* show, presumably to talk about upcoming fashion trends. When I checked *TV Guide* (at my boyfriend's insistence) and found out the show was to be about celebrity gossip, I backed out. I had other clients, but all anyone wanted to know about was Whitney Houston. I nevertheless did not discuss her or any of my clients with anyone. But some people could be persistent, obsessed even.

One afternoon, I received a strange call from a man who said his name was Wellington Houston. Sounding pretentious, he said, "I'm Whitney Houston's cousin and the people at her company referred me to you." When I asked for names he ignored me and asked, "What will it cost to hire Quietfire to do my makeup?"

"Well, what do you need grooming for?" I asked.

Once again he ignored my question and repeated, "Whitney's people referred me."

"Leave your name and number," I said. "I'll check Quietfire's availability and call you back." I called Nippy, Inc. immediately. When Donna Houston said the man was in no way affiliated with them, I simply forgot about the matter—until I received another call a week later.

"Hi, this is Wellington Houston. I'm still interested in Quietfire doing my make up." I told him Quietfire was out of town.

She Can Go Where Pretty Girls Go

Nevertheless, he called back the following day. He began calling once a week, then gradually three or four times a week. I usually said I was on another line or simply hung up. When I voiced my concern to Quietfire, he didn't seem to think there was a problem.

"Has your stalker called yet?" he'd tease. It wasn't funny to me. And it would become even less so.

One day my building's security called from the front desk to announce a visitor. "There's a Wellington Houston to see you. Shall I send him up?"

"No!" I answered quickly, trying not to panic. "Under no circumstances are you to let him up!" Thank goodness my boyfriend was there with me.

Bas grabbed the intercom and instructed security, "Get a full description!"

I called Donna at Nippy, Inc. She said the man had been going around telling people he was Whitney's cousin and had contacted the singer's hairstylist as well. "I'll have Whitney's head of security call you back," she promised. He called immediately saying the man was extremely dangerous and becoming a big problem for Whitney.

"Now *you* have a major problem," he added.

"What should I do?" I asked.

He simply replied, "Wellington is crazy and dangerous!"

I decided to go to the police. My building's security gave me a description of the man: "Well dressed, long hair weave, and he seemed gay." They also reported that he was riding in a black stretch limousine. Though intrigued by my story, the police said they could do nothing unless I was physically harmed. When Bas and I returned home, security informed us, "He came again while you were out." After that incident, I became more careful entering and leaving the building. Wellington called a few more times. After I began to threaten him, he stopped calling altogether. Later

Style Architect

I saw a BET newscast about Wellington and his frightening fixation with Whitney. He had been stalking her for some time and something was finally being done about it. "How must it be for celebrities to live in such fear on a regular basis," I wondered. I was horrified when Quietfire joked that he had gone behind my back and taken a booking from the stalker. At least I *think* he was joking.

Although Whitney was certainly Style Architect's biggest client, we were working with many other celebrities, including singers Freddy Jackson, Teddy Pendergrass, Peabo Bryson, Patti LaBelle, Nina Simone, and Jade as well as rappers Kwame and Father MC. My fashion clientele was growing as well. It included the house of Balenciaga, Chloe, St. John, Dennis Basso Furs, Ben Kahn Furs, Charles Jourdan, Ronaldus Shamask, Saks Fifth Avenue, J.C. Penney, Randolph Duke, Mark Eisen, and the legendary Adolfo.

As my company's reputation grew, calls from makeup artists, hairstylists, and fashion stylists flooded the office. Always on the lookout for talent, one day out of the month was set aside to view portfolios. Most were good but usually lacked that special something. In addition, I didn't accept anyone who didn't have a following of big-name clients. If so, they became "secondaries" and only did fill-in work. I needed someone special.

While walking to the Broadway and 96th Street subway station, on our way to Arista Records, Quietfire and I ran into an acquaintance of his. In his late twenties, tall, slim, and handsome with close-cut wavy hair and sideburns, the man introduced himself to me as "John Kellman-Grier, make up and hair. You're beautiful!" he added for good measure.

"Thank you," I smiled. He smiled back, firmly planted his fist on his side then got right down to business.

"I've heard a lot about you and I *really* need an agent," he said. "I'm swamped with work and it's become almost impossible trying to handle both the creative *and* business sides of my career."

"Give me a call later and we'll discuss it," I said. We exchanged business cards. I had a good feeling about John. He seemed honest and sincere—and had clients. It also helped that Quietfire vouched for him. He liked John and, feeling John's strong point was hair and his makeup, wouldn't feel threatened by his presence at Style Architect. John phoned that evening, making it official.

Since my new hair-and-makeup person lived just around the corner, we visited frequently and power-lunched at least twice a week. Generous, thoughtful, and real—that was John. He was respected and liked by everyone, especially me. He was always surprising me with gifts for my apartment and insisted on giving me a bonus for every job I booked for him. "You work hard for me," he said "You deserve it." John was also a perfectionist and the image of Style Architect was very important to him. "Presentation is everything, Miss Constance!"

Talent, attention to detail, and hard drive made John one of the most sought after beauty talents in the business. *Ebony Man* used him almost exclusively for their men's wear spreads. Singer Lisa Fisher was also keeping him busy. Another client was recording star Pebbles, who had started her own management company, Pebbitone, and wanted John for a brand-new girl act she was representing. The name of the trio was TLC, initials for T Boz, Left Eye, and Chili. The launch of their first single "Ain't Too Proud to Beg" and follow-up video shot the girls into stardom so quickly it boggled the mind.

But TLC weren't the only girl trio to book John. RCA's Jackie Murphy hired him as hairstylist for a new girl group *they* had signed. Needing a makeup artist as well, I suggested Quietfire. She booked both for an album cover and video shoot and gave

Style Architect

me a rundown on the group, a trio named SWV, short for Sisters With Voices. "These sustahs can sang!" proclaimed Jackie. She wanted an urban glam look for the Brooklyn threesome: Leann, Taj, and lead Coco, whose haunting voice sounded as good live as on tape. Also unique were her extraordinary long fingernails, elaborately painted and curved downward at the tips.

SWV became a huge hit after the release of their first single, "Right Here," from the debut album, *It's About Time*. We were booked for all their concert dates, publicity shoots, videos, television appearances, and award shows. Their third single "Weak" rocketed to number one on the pop charts and when the album went platinum, RCA celebrated with a big bash and guest list that included the top names in hip hop, including rapper TuPac Shakur. Quietfire and I attended. John didn't.

Even though things couldn't have been better work-wise, I was beginning to worry about John. When we started working together (nearly two years earlier) he was robust. Now he seemed unhealthy, was tiring easily. And as he was already thin, I became concerned when he started losing weight and taking long impromptu naps whenever he visited. "You need to start eating better and taking vitamins," I suggested.

"You're right, Miss Constance, you're right," he agreed. It was no use advising him to slow down. We were all working at a neck-breaking pace. I hadn't had any time off since I started the business. I became more concerned as John's behavior started to change. When he began requesting payment for jobs he already been paid for, I had to start making him sign for checks. His peculiar behavior was beginning to affect business.

John was booked with singer Kenny "Babyface" Edmunds and Antonio "LA" Reid, co-owners of LaFace Records, for a MTV spot. Having hit big in a duet with Babyface, he would be doing singer

She Can Go Where Pretty Girls Go

Toni Braxton's makeup as well. John refused the job and offered no explanation. "I'm busy, Miss Constance. Give it to Quiet," he said.

Thinking I must have heard him wrong, I asked, "What did you say?"

He repeated, "I said give it to Quiet." Which is exactly what I did. Since John was starting to miss assignments, I switched his more important clients over to Quietfire, including already scheduled bookings with LaFace artists, TLC.

I really became concerned when John's odd behavior cost us a huge account. Having worked with black opera diva Kathleen Battle for over a year and a half, he was booked to do the temperamental star's makeup for a live televised performance at Carnegie Hall. On the night of the scheduled booking I turned on the TV to see John's makeup and to hear Kathleen. Less than forty-five minutes before she was to perform, my phone rang. It was Michaela Kurz from Battle's management calling from backstage at Carnegie Hall. She sounded exasperated. "Kathleen goes on soon and John refuses to do her makeup!" she said. "What am I supposed to do now?"

"What do you mean, he refuses to do her makeup?" I asked, "What happened?"

"I don't know, Constance! He just refuses to do it!"

Trying to remain calm myself, I advised her, "Please calm down and put him on the phone." When John got on the phone he acted as if nothing was wrong.

"What's up, Miss Constance?"

"What's the problem John?"

"Problem? Pleazzze! Miss Kathleen's not the only diva in the house. Right, girl?" I was so upset I couldn't answer. With little time left before the concert started, I was desperate to snatch John back into reality.

Style Architect

Through clenched teeth, I said, "John, If you don't do your job, like the professional I know you are, I'm coming straight down to Carnegie Hall and kicking your ass *up* and down the concert aisles! Now try me!" I threatened. Amazingly, it worked.

"Yes, Miss Constance, you're right, girl. I'm going to punch Miss Kathleen's face lovely!"

Relieved, I answered, "Only you can." When the operatic star appeared, she looked breathtaking and sang beautifully. Understandably though, we never heard from her again.

No longer able to attribute John's strange behavior, lack of strength, or weight loss to exhaustion, I demanded he get a physical exam. "When I get a free moment," he said for the umpteenth time. He visited early one morning to hang out and of course, talk business. Within twenty-minutes he was stretched out on my living room floor, fast asleep. Eight hours passed before he finally woke up and composed himself.

"John you're going to have to see a doctor!" I demanded.

"I promise you I will, Miss Constance. Soon as I get a free moment." Nearly three months later he got so sick he had no choice.

John was rushed to Cabrini Hospital in downtown Manhattan, where he was admitted. When I spoke with him over the phone he said matter-of-factly, "I've been diagnosed with tuberculosis and cancer." Devastated, Quietfire and I strongly suspected our beloved coworker and friend suffered from complications caused by AIDS. When my boyfriend Bas and I visited John in the hospital, his gaunt gray appearance left little doubt that the disease had claimed one of our own.

My ex-boss Audrey Smaltz had recently lost her friend and in house makeup artist Al Grundy. Barbara Bennett was still mourning the loss of her dear friend James Finney, renowned hairstylist for *The Cosby Show*. Celebrated designer Patrick Kelly's death

She Can Go Where Pretty Girls Go

stunned the fashion world. A dark cloud loomed over the fashion and beauty industries. Many of its best talents were sick, dying, or dead. The cloud had finally drifted over Style Architect. I put on a smile whenever I visited John at the hospital but once home, I broke down. After his release, I visited him at his apartment. Wearing a ton of makeup to mask the illness and with some sort of tube in his chest, John was talking as if nothing had happened, making grand plans for his return to work. It absolutely broke my heart.

John's health deteriorated so quickly, he decided to return to his hometown in Indiana to be with his family. We spoke over the phone every day. Discussing the past and his return to Style Architect, his spirits were sky-high. I was totally unprepared and numbed when he passed away only a few weeks after leaving New York. John was only thirty-two.

I was turning forty on May 21, 1993 and decided to give myself a party. I invited forty coworkers and friends, including Alvaro, Barbara Bennett, Quietfire, and Kim, who brought her new boyfriend (and future husband), whom she met seven months earlier on a Caribbean cruise. The night before the party I had a moving dream about my recently departed friend John. We were walking up a steep street in Spanish Harlem when he turned to me and said, "Just in case you want to know, Miss Contance, there *is* a God." We continued walking until we reached a large elevator at the top of the street. The door opened and John stepped in. "You're going to be a much bigger success," he said right before the elevator door closed. I woke up crying. It was the last time I ever spoke with John. His passing left an enormous void, both professionally and personally.

By 1995 I was growing tired of a life that rotated around business. I wanted to spend more time on my personal life and give more attention to my boyfriend and friends. I didn't have many

Style Architect

friends outside of business. Jackie and I had fallen out of touch again and it had been six years since I last saw her. Our friendship was never quite the same after I moved out of her apartment under unfavorable circumstances in 1985. We had seen each other since then and even worked together on a few fashion shows but lost touch soon afterwards. Kim was the only real friend I had outside Style Architect. Even though she had left Manhattan, I visited as much as possible. She was married to a successful businessman and pregnant with her first child. Most of her time was spent decorating her new thirteen-room home in Verona, New Jersey, preparing for motherhood, and becoming the perfect trophy wife. Whenever our busy schedules allowed she would come into the city and we would shop midtown, lunch in Soho, or have cocktails at the Shark Bar on the Upper-West-Side.

I especially needed more personal time with my boyfriend. Retired from the MTA, Bas helped out with the company and worked with Jazzmobile during the summers. We were doing well financially. He received a nice retirement package and Style Architect was a big success. I had three bank accounts and a self-earned A1 credit rating. My closet was filled with beautiful and expensive clothes, bags, and accessories by Chanel, and footwear from Manolo Blanik. And I was no longer riding the dark smelly subways: a private car service became my new mode of transportation. We also moved into a much larger apartment. Located on the twenty-fourth floor in the same building, the garden terrace offered a panoramic view of the Manhattan skyline and Central Park. With things going so well, I should have felt great. But something was missing.

In the beginning, things were good between Bas and me. He had provided the foundation on which I rebuilt my life. Determined to be successful, I became so preoccupied with work I paid little attention to anything else, including our relationship. I

She Can Go Where Pretty Girls Go

hadn't even paid much attention to his lack of affection toward me. I believed Bas loved me; he just wasn't used to showing affection (other than during sex), something I was starting to want and need. Over time it got to me. When confronted, Bas became defensive and sarcastic. "What do you want me to do, walk around holding you all day?" If forced, he'd give me an emotionless, quickie bear hug and walk away. An argument usually ensued. It got to a point where we were arguing practically every Sunday, my only day off from work.

After awhile we tired of constantly arguing and agreed to try and accept each other, as is. Either we were going to continue bickering and eventually break up or work together on our problems. Things did get a little better. Though somewhat awkwardly, Bas even tried being affectionate occasionally. And on November 1, 1995, after eight years of living together, he actually proposed. It wasn't very romantic. He just said, "I think we should be married. In case something happened to me, you'll be provided for. Who knows how long Style Architect will last." It was a good enough reason for me. I loved Bas and felt I needed some sort of security. I would just try to deal with the affection issue as best I could. Bas and I got married four days after his proposal, on November 5th at Manhattan's City Hall. Neither of us wanted anything fancy. We just wanted to get married. After the ceremony we came home, shared a bottle of Taittinger, made love, then went right back to work on a booking for Whitney Houston.

After six years, I lost my biggest client, Whitney Houston. After using Quietfire on her movie, *Waiting To Exhale*, an extremely lucrative three-month gig, she booked him for several movie promotions (including the *Oprah Winfrey* show) as well as an album cover for the movie soundtrack. When the star started work on her next film, *The Preacher's Wife*, she only used him for the screen test. For the movie she chose someone else, costar Angela

Style Architect

Bassett's make up artist for *Waiting To Exhale*. The following year we also lost SWV as clients when Keith Hayes (the group's hairstylist since John's death) and I refused to a rate reduction for the first video to their follow-up album, *New Beginning*. The girls phoned complaining, "Everybody's trying to get rich off the S, the W, and the V!" Soon afterward they parted ways with their manager, and eventually with one another.

Quietfire and I parted ways as well. I got angry when he went behind my back and tried to convince a new makeup artist not to be represented by me. There had been other things—but mainly, I needed a change. We had eight years together, good times and bad. I learned so much from Quietfire and respected him as one of the most talented and hardest working people in the business.

Even though I had lost my two most lucrative clients and parted ways with one of my most talented artists, I was busier than ever. I had a new make up artist named Aliesh Pierce, whose clients included singers Monifah, Amel Larrieux of the duo "Groove Theory", and Shanice. Also, Keith was still with me. Jive Records hired him to create a new look for jazz artist Marion Meadows. They also booked him to work with a new boy group, Backstreet Boys. A stylist named June Ambrose was hired to dress the group. She was making a name for herself working with rap tycoon Sean "Puffy" Combs and his stable of "Bad Boy" artists. Keith convinced the stylist to join Style Architect. She was booked almost daily with artists like Backstreet Boys, 69 Boyz, David Hollister, and Missy Elliott among others. A *Rolling Stone* cover featuring Sean Combs was booked through Style Architect as well. We were working more than ever—so much that there was little time for anything else. I was burnt out and needed a break.

She Can Go Where Pretty Girls Go

Left to right: Singer Whitney Houston, producer Narada Michael Walden, and Walden's brother at Whitney's twenty-sixth birthday bash.

Gospel singer Bebe Winans at Whitney's party.

Style Architect

Me lounging in tent at Whitney's party.

Singer Dionne Warwick and birthday girl.

She Can Go Where Pretty Girls Go

Singer Lisa Fisher with Style Architect hairstylist and makeup artist, John Kellman-Grier.

Me in the New York Times fashion section, photographed leaving the Plaza Hotel where I worked on Adolfo fashion show.

Artist Spenser Michaels and his beautiful agent at *Nuts & Bolts*

Artist Spencer Michaels and me in a New York magazine.

Style Architect

Caught taking a quickie nap.

She Can Go Where Pretty Girls Go

A family reunited. Left to right: Sister Ernestine, brother Mario, sister Deb, brother Lester, and me in Carlisle, S.C. for Mama Annie Bell's funeral.

After a long day working on *She Can Go Where Pretty Girls Go*, sister Deb and me celebrating my fiftieth birthday in New York City on May 21, 2003.

LIFE'S HALL OF FAME

Mom had been living in Carlisle, South Carolina, since her mother suffered her first stoke in the late seventies. Her eldest sister and my favorite aunt, Gertrude, joined her shortly afterwards and remained there until her untimely death at fifty-six. After the initial stroke, my grandmother didn't get around as well but still had all her faculties. By the late eighties she had suffered another stroke, which left her semicomatose. Over the next eight years Mom devoted herself to caring for Mama Annie Bell. But in 1995 I received a heartbreaking phone call. "Mama jus' passed!" cried my mother, so hard she could barely speak. "Pa—please, Connie, call Lester and Deb for me." One hundred years old, Mama Annie Bell was my last surviving grandparent (Paternal grandparents Eula Bell and Allen had died two years earlier, one right after the other). Mom was with her when she passed on, as was my eldest sister who had driven up from her home in Atlanta, Georgia. Ernestine was inconsolable. Our grandmother had raised her. My brother Mario was already down South, having lived there for the past five years. After giving Lester and Deb the bad news, I made arrangements to fly to Carlisle.

I was one of the first out-of-town family members to arrive, picked up at the airport by my cousin Travis Crosby. It felt strange

She Can Go Where Pretty Girls Go

being back. I hadn't been in Carlisle since I left at age nine. After checking on Mom, visiting with my sister Ernestine and my brother Mario, I took a long walk, alone. Strangely, I knew my way around. Some things had changed. Gone were the dirt roads, the farms, the pastures of animals, the white-only schoolhouse that use to sit near the ball field, and the old train depot with the "colored" and "white only" signs. But mostly things looked and felt the same: the water tower bearing the town's name, the old general store on Fishdam Road, the breathtaking countryside, the people, and the houses. The antebellum mansion was still there. Even the old tin-roofed house I grew up in was still standing. As I peeked in the window, I could almost see Grandma Eula Bell, Granddaddy, my brother, sister, and myself laughing as we roasted sweet potatoes in the fireplace.

Mama Annie Bell's house, where my mother lived, turned out to be not as scary as I had remembered. The "back room," which had remained locked for over twenty-five years because of supposed ghost sightings, was now open. Mom used it as a pantry. Even though not frightened by the room, sometimes I still caught a chill whenever I passed. Mostly though, the house felt comforting. And I needed my mother as much as she needed me.

Understandably, Mom wasn't doing well. She cried nonstop for three days. "I 'on know what to do wit' myself," she complained. Now sixty-two, her life had revolved around the care of her mother. No stranger to a party, Mom still drank and hosted card parties, but she had diligently cared for her mother. Mama Annie Bell rarely had a bedsore and even at one hundred, had a smooth, clear complexion. Mom missed her terribly. "I wake up in the middle of the night and look over at her bed to check on her. Then I remember. My mama not here no mo'," she sobbed.

Over the next few days, family arrived. In from Portland, Oregon, beautiful and radiant under a waterfall of golden dreads that hung to her waist, Deb wept on and off for five days. As well as feeling sad at our grandmother's passing, now thirty-nine with two grown daughters and three grandchildren, Daniel, Reeonlanae, and Jontel, she was experiencing an unexpected feeling of roots. I was so happy to see her, I cried too. Though we spoke by phone no less than four times a week, I had only seen my younger sister twice over the past ten years, when I visited Portland in 1992 and when she came to New York the following year. Along with my two sisters and brother, it was also good to see my Aunts Edna, Elneder, and Geraldine and all their children, grandchildren, and great-grandchildren. My late Auntie Gertrude's only child Mary Ferguson had moved from Cleveland, Ohio to Carlisle a few years earlier and lived just up the road from my mother. Her daughter and my favorite cousin Patricia, along with toddlers Tatiana and Butchie, joined her shortly afterwards. Mom's only surviving brother, Uncle Mack, had also moved back from Columbus, Ohio, but for reasons unknown to anyone but him, refused to attend his own mother's funeral. (Brothers Henry, LC, and Crenshaw were deceased, the latter killed in the late thirties when police, shooting at a suspect, missed and shot him instead.) It felt strange but good being surrounded by family. Though most of them hadn't seen me since I was a child, they treated me as if I had been Constance from birth.

My older brother Lester arrived at the eleventh hour, just as the family gathered on the front porch waiting for the limousines that were to take us to the funeral. "This the first time all my kids been togetha since 1975," wept Mom as she hugged her son tightly. The funeral service, held at the same church we attended as children, was simple. Mama Annie Bell was laid to rest in an open pink, angel-accented casket. She looked amazing for a hundred-year-old woman who was deceased. My father's oldest sister Irene sang. Reverend Worthy preached an old-fashioned down-home sermon. In it, he praised Mom's dedication to her mother. There wasn't a dry eye in AME Methodist. My first cousin Valerie wailed heartbreakingly throughout the entire service. Mom took it worse. Near collapse, she had to be helped to and from the casket. Though Mama Annie Bell would certainly be missed by all of us, she left a void in my mother's life that would never be filled.

I stayed in Carlisle longer than the rest of the family to help Mom take care of Mama Annie Bell's estate. Also I got a chance to visit with relatives on my father's side. A cousin, Janie Glymph-Goree, my childhood babysitter and, in 1978, the first black female elected to the office of Mayor in the state of South Carolina, stopped in to give her condolences. A retired high school math teacher, she entertained us with stories of her visits to the White House and political dealings with the likes of Senator Strom Thurmond. My father's sister Eula Mae also stopped by. All too soon it was time to return home. I had been in Carlisle for two weeks and it was near impossible trying to conduct business from there. I was needed back in New York.

I returned to Carlisle a year later to help Mom with my grandmother's estate, just out of probate. She inherited two of the four acres her parents Douglas and Annie Bell Crosby purchased in the early forties, and seventeen acres of family land settled by her grandparents George and Abbey Cofield. In appreciation of my moral and financial support during the time she cared for her mother, Mom gave me an acre and a half of breathtaking wooded property, a piece of family history.

Even though I had planned for some much-needed relaxation in Carlisle's tranquil setting, it was almost impossible to get any rest at Mom's. She and her live-in boyfriend (twenty-two years her junior) liked entertaining. The house was often crowded with people drinking and playing cards until dawn. Attending to business was challenging as well. We had to ride fifteen miles to the

Life's Hall of Fame
_____

Union County Courthouse to take care of property transactions. An old friend of my father's, Doc Pony drove us in his old blue Ford pickup, the town's only taxi service. "I'd reconize you anywhere, Connie. You the spittin' image of yo daddy," he laughed.

It wasn't easy gaining entrance to the courthouse because the biggest story that ever hit Union County was unfolding inside. One of Union's own, Susan Smith was on trial for the drowning deaths of her two small children. It was national news. Smith had originally lied, alleging her children had been abducted by a black man during a car-jacking. "Police came through here questionin' ev'rybody," complained one male Carlisle resident.

"They even arrested a man over in Monarch they said looked like the one Susan Smith described!" another man angrily added. Smith eventually confessed to the horrific crime and was being tried in the very courthouse where we had gone to take care of Mom's business. The atmosphere surrounding the stately 136-year-old building was circus-like. Several television stations had platforms built in front for better viewing, making it virtually impossible to walk on the sidewalks. Spectators also crowded the sidewalks as proceedings from inside the courtroom blared out into the street over loudspeakers. When we finally got inside the building a white lady who looked to be around my mother's age approached her.

"Hi, Effie, it's been so long. Betcha don't remember me." After a few blank seconds, Mom recognized the lady to be Mrs. Smith, mother-in-law to the accused killer and grandmother of the slain children.

"I remember you. Remember ya son David too. Use ta cut Mama's grass sometimes," said Mom. Mrs. Smith gave her condolences for Mom's loss. My mother offered words of comfort to the grieving grandmother. On a break from proceedings, Mrs. Smith returned solemnly to the courtroom. Mom and I took care of business, maneuvered our way past the mob outside then headed back to Carlisle.

Aside from the Smith trial the small town was so tranquil I contemplated building a house on the land Mom had given me. It would be ideal after the hectic pace of Manhattan. On the plane back to New York, the idea of owning a house began to appeal to me even more. I was roasted from working sixteen-hour days for over ten years and needed to start thinking more about my personal life; about family; about friends.

Jim Stallard and I had been friends since dancing on the *Upbeat* television show during the late sixties and early seventies. Along with his dance partner Bev Jones, we were together so much back then we were nicknamed the Mod Squad. In 1971, after Bev died tragically in an auto crash and *Upbeat* got cancelled, I didn't see much of Jim. He finished college and began teaching school and I started my new life as Connie. He had kept in touch periodically over the years but recently started phoning regularly, about three times a week. He also sent several videotapes of then-current television specials about *Upbeat* featuring interviews with the dancers. A great interest in the show had redeveloped since Cleveland was chosen as the site for the Rock and Roll Hall of Fame. An *Upbeat* calendar and weekly planner was published in 1996 with a history of the show and pictures of a parade of pop, rock, and rhythm-and-blues stars. A picture of me appeared in the book alongside fellow dancers. Having destroyed all pictures of me taken before 1971, it felt strange seeing myself as I was over thirty years ago. He had been a closely guarded secret for most of my life and now suddenly, Arlee was on television again. Still, I felt a sense of pride that something done so long ago was still being viewed and enjoyed. So did Jim.

Jim invited me to visit his Cleveland suburban home. Though we spoke on the phone regularly I hadn't seen him since 1980,

Life's Hall of Fame

fifteen years earlier. The timing was perfect. I needed to renew my Ohio driver's license and would have to be in Cleveland anyway. During my visit, I stayed with my brother Lester and his family at their beautiful University Heights home. My first day there I got a surprise visitor. Lester heard a car door slam in his driveway and looked out to see. His forehead furrowed. "That's strange," he said. "It's Walter! He's never visited me before." Walter was my mother's live-in boyfriend and the man of our house for most of my childhood. Looking a lot older and frailer than the last time I saw him, more than fifteen years earlier, Walter slowly made his way inside and came straight over to me. Then he totally surprised me with a hug.

"I heard you was in town and had to come by and see you." Then with utmost sincerity he said, "I'm sorry for how I treated you when you was a child." I almost cried and so did he. Walter took a seat and, along with my brother, his wife Sandra, and me, laughed and talked for the rest of the afternoon. He even stayed for dinner. We had an enjoyable evening, and I was especially glad we made our peace. Sadly though, Walter died a few months later. I was grateful for the chance to see him. A chance I didn't get with my biological father, Arlee Sr., before his death a year earlier. I hadn't seen him since I was nine or spoken to him since the age of sixteen. He was living in Washington, D.C., at the time, and after seeing me on television, phoned then mailed me twenty dollars. I never heard from him again. One of my few regrets is not seeing him before his death.

Driving a new SUV, Jim picked me up from my brother's my third day in town to spend some time at his house. On the way he made a detour to my old childhood neighborhood in the projects—much uglier and more depressing than I had remembered. Jim wanted to sit in the pot-holed parking lot and reminisce. I wanted to get as far away from the place as possible.

She Can Go Where Pretty Girls Go

After a very brief tour of the old hood, we headed west to Jim's house. Located just off Lake Shore Boulevard, the impressive three-story brick Colonial sat on a vast wooded corner lot. After a tour of his Early American-decorated home, we retired to the media room where Jim reminisced as we watched old *Upbeat* videotapes transferred from even older 8-mm film. Added attractions were home movies of his family in the early fifties and footage of his former *Upbeat* dance partner and our mutual friend Bev Jones.

Following the home movies, we had a late supper in the breakfast room, decorated with beautiful large stained-glass windows. After the gourmet meal, cooked and graciously served by Jim's roommate Frank, I was ready for bed. My accommodations were four-star: the entire third floor, which included a sitting room, large sunny bath, and terraced bedroom. On my pillow lay two current fashion magazines and Godiva chocolates, provided by my thoughtful hosts.

I awoke early to the blaring sounds of Gloria Estefan and the Miami Sound Machine and the aroma of freshly brewed coffee. A knock on the door was followed with Frank's announcement: "Breakfast is being served out on the deck!" Throughout the entire meal Jim and I remembered and laughed.

Then in a serious tone, Jim said, "Connie, It's great seeing you. It's been way too long. I want you to know how proud I am of you, of everything you've done and the person you've become." I was proud of him as well. After college he became a teacher, working in the inner city where he felt most needed. Following an early retirement, he ran a successful upholstery business with his roommate Frank and coached a high school girl's soccer team part time. He also maintained a two-family home purchased years earlier. But lately, most of Jim's time had been spent enjoying his beautiful Colonial and supervising construction on a new

Life's Hall of Fame

swimming pool. "You must promise me that you'll come to my pool party when the pool is finished in a couple of months," he smiled.

"Of course!" I said. "I wouldn't miss it for anything." As much as I hated to, nearly an hour after breakfast, it was time for me to leave.

Jim and Frank pleaded with me to "Stayyy! At least one more day!"

"I'd love to," I said, "But today's my brother's birthday and his wife's having a cookout to celebrate."

"At least stay long enough so we can take pictures!" Frank demanded as he headed inside for the camera. It was fabulous spending time with Jim. We agreed we needed to see each other more often. On the plane back to New York I drifted off thinking about the old days with Jim, Bev, and me: the Mod Squad.

Jim and I kept in frequent touch over the next few months. He began traveling and sent postcards from every port. When he returned home, we talked on the phone almost every evening. Then abruptly, without any explanation, he stopped calling. I was concerned and began phoning practically every day for three weeks, leaving messages on his answering machine. But he never returned my calls. That was unlike Jim. Upon returning home one night from an industry party I had attended with my friend Alvaro, my husband greeted me at the door with a dark look of concern. "What?" I asked. He slowly led me to the sofa and sat me down. "What?" I repeated louder.

"Now don't lose it," he pleaded. Then he walked over to my desk and played back a message on the answering machine.

"Hi Connie, this is Frank. Our Jimmie's gone. He passed away this morning." When I started screaming Bas grabbed and held me tightly. After about twenty minutes I calmed down just long enough to call Frank.

191

She Can Go Where Pretty Girls Go

"Prior to Jim going into the hospital I didn't even know he was sick," said Frank. Jim had apparently kept his illness a secret from everyone. I asked what he had died from but Frank was vague. Months earlier, Jim had sent me a videotape of himself being interviewed on an *Upbeat* special. I was shocked by his gray gaunt appearance, but wrote it off as his not aging well. And when I visited him he looked a lot better, like his old self.

"I wished he had told me he was sick. We could have spent more time together," I cried to Bas. Jim had been my friend since I was fifteen-years-old and had kept in contact with me through every phase of my life. Searching for some kind of comfort, I imagined my friend in heaven dancing with his *Upbeat* partner and dear friend Bev.

Jim's death was handled like most personal crises during that time, working harder with plans to deal with it later, when I could better handle it. Eventually the pace got to me. I desperately needed some time off and a completely different setting. I had saved some money and decided the best investment would be in a house. It could be built on my land down South. As well as getting some much-needed rest, I would also get the chance to be around my family for a while. I hadn't spent very much time with them over the past fifteen years.

Flying back and forth from New York to Carlisle, building my home was a monumental project. As well as designing it, I was on site with the construction crew as often as possible to ensure that everything was done to my specifications. After a year of planning and six months of construction, my house was finally completed. "Yo house is tight!" shouted a handsome young man in sagging jeans as he walked by. I totally agreed. It was just as I had imagined. The sand-colored brick structure was given a stately look by adding an impressive A-framed porch supported by white classical Greek columns. The living room, dining room, and kitchen floors were covered in light oak hardwood and all three bedrooms in wheat-colored carpeting. Crystal chandeliers hung in the living and dining rooms and numerous large windows allowed for maximum lighting and viewing.

I loved my new house but the main attraction was the beautiful grounds. The house was surrounded on three sides by giant trees, mostly cedar, oak, and pine. A Greek statue of a partially nude woman and large stone planters dotted the vast back yard. A stone patio with lion-head benches and marble tables was a great spot from which to view two eye-catching peacocks housed in a large pen nearby. A path, made through the ivy ground-covered woods behind the backyard, led past a seventeenth-century cemetery (the same one that spooked me as a child) to the bantam rooster pen. It also led up to the railroad tracks where I had a bird's eye view of my family's seventeen forested acres. After thirteen years in the break-neck-not-a-minute-to-waste business of fashion, beauty, and music, my home was a place of relaxation and tranquility. (By 1999 I stopped Style Architect altogether and spent most of my time at my home in Carlisle, while my hard-core New Yorker husband remained in the city.) Unfortunately though, my tranquil setting was about to explode.

Though there were a few kind souls in town, my reception was less than welcoming by some. By way of a close relative, word had gotten out that Connie was once Arlee, whom surprisingly a few remembered. One of my worst fears was finally being realized: I was in a place where everyone knew my business. And they weren't shy about expressing themselves either. There were incidents of name-calling. A man yelled, "Show me your balls!" as I walked past the park.

A group of children sang, "That's Effie's daughter, she is a man!" as I drove by one day.

She Can Go Where Pretty Girls Go

And a close family member got ugly-drunk and said I was "nothing but a man turned into a woman." It all hurt—deeply! All came to a head when, on New Years Day, 2000, I went with my brother Mario to the only bar in town.

A man whom I refused to buy a drink for called me, of all things, a "Punk!"

"What did you say?" I asked, double-checking. He repeated it, only this time a little nastier. That was it! I grabbed the wooden barstool next to me, and with one hand hurled it at the man's head. It found its mark and he fell to the floor. Two additional stools followed—each also finding their marks.

"Brotha caught a beat down!" yelled a husky-voiced dark-skinned woman. Others rushed to the fallen man's aid. Luckily, he was more dazed than hurt. Extremely shaken myself, I rushed to my car and sped home. My keys shaking, I steadied my hand just long enough to unlock the door. Once inside, I collapsed to the floor bawling and screaming.

"What am I doing? Have I gone crazy? I could've seriously hurt someone!" While I lay on the floor for nearly two hours crying, images of me brawling flooded my head. It was a horrifying experience, one that would force me to deal with many things, including my past.

With people in town and family knowing my business, I was forced to think about my life as Arlee, something I hadn't given much thought to over the past thirty-something years. "How am I going to deal with people knowing?" I asked myself aloud? No longer able—or even willing—to hide, I would also have to deal with telling my husband. "That would be difficult," I thought. "*Extremely* difficult. What would I say?" I called my sister Deb (now married to an engineer and attending college in St. Petersburg, Florida) for advice. She wasn't home. I was partially in tears when I called Bas that same night and told him.

"I totally understand if you want a divorce," I said. At first he was silent.

Then he said, "I don't know what you're talking about. All I know you as is Constance, my wife." When I tried to discuss it further, he interrupted, "We don't need to talk anymore about it," and quickly changed the subject. I was elated that Bas took everything so amazingly well. Nevertheless, *I* still needed to talk about it—at least to myself. In search of a way to express my feelings, I grabbed a pen and tablet and started writing—about everything: about my father abandoning me, about my career as a dancer, about my gender problem and resolution. Going over the good memories brought comfort and smiles; going over the bad, pain and tears. Before I knew it, I was writing a book. As time went on my writing began to help me get through and deal with a lot: my marriage, recent deaths, family, and friends. It also helped me to deal with my past and people's reaction to it. Eventually the town got used to me and stopped treating me like an outsider. I on the other hand, never got completely used to them and kept pretty much to myself. I continued working on my book and kept in daily contact with my husband, my sister Deb, and my best friend Kim.

In April 2000 I got a phone call from my friend Kim with a message from my estranged friend Jackie requesting I phone immediately on a matter of great importance. Kim was doing well, happily married with two beautiful sons and living in New Jersey. After a two-year hiatus she was back working for Chanel part-time. "Go ahead and call Jackie, Constance," said Kim. "And call me as soon as you're done talking. I'm curious as to what's so urgent after all these years." I hadn't spoken to Jackie in eleven years. As I dialed her number I was nervous, thinking something bad might had happened. But her news was amazing.

She Can Go Where Pretty Girls Go

"You have to go to Cleveland immediately!" said Jackie. "*Upbeat*'s being honored at the Rock and Roll Hall of Fame. Also, the WEWS television station is being made a landmark because *Upbeat* was taped there. The ceremonies are being held day after tomorrow and you *have* to be there!"

"Of course I'm coming!" I said. "I haven't seen you in eleven years. And I haven't seen the people from *Upbeat* in over *thirty* years!" The last time most of them saw me I was a seventeen-year-old boy. "How will they take to me as a forty-six-year-old woman?" I wondered.

I was exhausted when I arrived at my downtown Cleveland hotel room. My brother Lester had offered his home, but the hotel was much closer to the WEWS-TV station and Rock and Roll Hall of Fame. There was little time before the first of three events honoring *Upbeat* was to begin. My first phone call was to my brother Lester. Then I called Jackie, who had just arrived from New York and was staying at her mom's. She had been accepted into a law school in Cleveland and was planning to move there temporarily. "I'm so proud of you," I said.

"Thanks! Constance, you know I'm not quite settled in yet," she said, "and I'm unsure of exactly what times the ceremonies start. So let me give you some of the other dancers phone numbers and I'll call and get the information from you when I get settled. I can't wait to see you."

"Me too," I answered.

Gail Philpott screamed, "I was afraid you wouldn't make it!" when I called her. Previously a local television personality, my first *Upbeat* dance partner taught telecommunications at her old high school. After a brief but happy phone reunion she gave me what little information she had. "Arline and Hank should know more. Remember we're family and we all love you, Constance," she assured me.

Life's Hall of Fame

I called Arline Burks next. "I'm so glad you came!" she said. "I can't wait to see you. I have the day's schedule but you might want to call Hank to double-check." Arline had done well for herself. She was a model in her youth. On hiatus from her job as a fashion stylist, she had worked on several movies and did a stint with the very popular *Martin* sitcom. She was married to actor Richard Gant and had a daughter named Dakota.

My last call was to Maurice "Hank" Nystom, *Upbeat*'s choreographer during its heyday. I was nervous as I dialed and relieved when his reception was warm and enthusiastic. Someone had already informed him that my name was Constance. "Do you prefer Connie?" he asked. I didn't. A good steady conversation, Hank and I talked for about fifteen minutes, mostly about the day's events and which dancers had and had not come. Surprisingly, none of the "main" male dancers showed up. Two had passed away: my dear friend Jim Stallard, and Michael Ray, who danced on the show during its last two years. Mysteriously, John Magill wasn't returning calls.

"I guess I'll be the only 'boy' dancer here Hank," I giggled. Always open for a joke, Hank laughed along. After talking for close to twenty minutes we hung up. Then I showered and hurried into a classic Chanel suit for the first event, starting in an hour.

Held outside in front of the WEWS-TV station, the landmark ceremony had already started when I arrived. TV cameras, photographers, and reporters crowded the sidewalk. The first familiar faces were Jackie and her mom, Mrs. Nicholson. Expertly made up with long loose curls and dressed in a black top, matching skin-tight pants, and Versace bag, Jackie was even prettier and younger looking than when I last saw her, eleven years ago. Amazingly, so was her mom. We embraced, but not before Mrs. Nicholson snatched off my sunglasses. "You're too pretty to hide your face!" she scolded. Mrs. Nicholson wanted me prepared for any photo ops. She was still the stage Mom she was during our dancing heyday.

Next I spotted Gail, calling out "Constance, over here!" as she motioned me to sit next to her in chairs set up for the outside ceremony. I was surprised she recognized me. I almost didn't recognize *her*. Gone were the big afro and mini dress, replaced by a conservative short haircut and suit. We only got a chance to speak briefly. Because when Hank (looking almost exactly as he did over thirty years ago) realized who I was, he swiftly scooped me up from my seat, insisting I say hello to former *Upbeat* host Don Webster.

Grinning, he asked Don, "Do you know who this is?" Don shook my hand as he struggled to remember. "I'll give you a hint," said Hank. "She's a former *Upbeat* dancer." Though he tried his best to remember my face, Don hadn't a clue. He slowly shook his head. Then finally Hank said, "It's Arlee, Don!" Don was visibly shocked but gracious as he welcomed me back. A snickering Hank absolutely *loved* it!

An array of *Upbeat* alumni was present for the plaque presentation including the Miracles, Ben E. King, Gene Chandler and Freda Payne, looking almost as ravishing as she did when I danced alongside her more than three decades earlier. Having successfully retrieved me from Hank, Jackie's mom carefully positioned her daughter and me where we had the best chance of being photographed. But it was difficult listening to all the long speeches so the first chance we got, Jackie and I slipped inside the studio to the ladies' room. It had been a long time since we last saw one another and there was quite a bit of catching-up to do. We didn't get very far though. Within three minutes Jackie's mom was in to fetch us. "What are you girls doing in here? They're taking pictures out there!" she scolded as she scooted us out. It

Life's Hall of Fame

was just like the old days: being at the station, seeing the old crowd, being treated like teenagers. As soon as we walked into the crowded reception area several cameras flashed at us. Jackie flashed back with that big perfect smile of hers and posed while I just stood there. When a hand tapped gently on the back of my shoulder, I quickly turned around.

"Excuse me. Can I speak to you for a minute?" a black female security guard asked politely.

"Sure," I answered, wondering what I had done.

"I'm sorry for disturbing you," she said. "But I'm an old fan of yours. We lived in the same neighborhood back when you were dancing and I just had to let you know that you made us all so proud back then, the entire projects. I just needed to thank you for that." Then she hugged me. I was so moved I almost cried. At that moment I gained a new sense of pride in my life as Arlee.

After a post-ceremony photo op, Jackie, her mom, and I headed straight to the Rock and Roll Hall of Fame where a special dinner was held in honor of the occasion. We joined Hank, his lovely wife Selena, and former dancer Jean Hagedorn at the dancer's table. Just as pretty as she was at sixteen, Jean leaned over and smiled at me. "I'm so pleased that you look so happy," she said. I *was* happy. It was like an incredible dream, being with my old *Upbeat* family as Constance and being honored by the Rock and Roll Hall of Fame. After dinner, cocktails, and more speeches I raced back to the hotel in a rented red Camaro to change for the final event. An *Upbeat* concert was scheduled at the Rock and Roll Hall of Fame featuring past guests. The dancers were asked to do a number as well. I decided on a more casual look: a cream beaded T-shirt, brown suede pants, matching boots, and a short denim jacket.

On the chilly Lake Erie shore where the Rock and Roll Hall of Fame was located, hundreds lined up outside, anxiously waiting to get in. I met Jackie and her mom just inside the main entrance.

She Can Go Where Pretty Girls Go

On our way upstairs, we ran into fellow dancer Linda Mulcahy-Fazio and her husband Bob (former member of *Upbeat* house band People's Choice), with their three teenagers. Linda looked fantastic, as slim as during her teens. She wore a tailored green pantsuit and her once long blonde mane was now a smart short cut. The very first thing she said to me was, "Can you still do the shiver?" my signature dance move back in the sixties.

I opened my jacket and responded, "I have absolutely too much chest for all that shaking." We laughed. "You look fabulous, girl," I said.

"Yeah," Linda replied, "but I wish I had that body!" Just then, Arline Burks-Gant walked over. We all giggled and hugged. "You look great, Constance!" said Arline, who was accompanied by her husband and daughter. Then she apologized for some weight gain but there was no need to. Tall, green-eyed, and with her hair snatched back in a long ponytail, Arline looked stunning. Then Gail Philpott joined us briefly before finding a place to sit. Overwhelmed by the days' event, I followed her moments later. Amidst the chaos, she was the most calm of the group. As she looked at an old picture of us that one of the dancers had handed her, Gail drifted.

"Remember, you and I were the ones who brought the popcorn [a dance] to the show," she said.

"Yeah, I remember." I smiled.

Finally, the enthusiastic crowd was let in. The concert area on the mezzanine level became quickly packed. People rushed over to speak with the dancers, who were congregated near the backstage. Some had old pictures of us. After a few minutes it hit me that the middle-aged crowd were our old fans, all grown up. It surprised me that they were still fans of a show that had been off the air for over three decades. I didn't know how, but some recognized me and came over to speak as if I was still Arlee. Even asked me to autograph old pictures of myself. Confused, I wondered if

Life's Hall of Fame

everyone had known about me all these years. No one seemed to notice that I had changed quite a bit—or even cared. Maybe it was never about gender. Maybe to them, Arlee was about that pure joy of movement that we all share as children. Though moving and possibly revealing, it was still a very weird experience.

After talking briefly with several old Upbeat fans, Hank summoned all the dancers backstage to rehearse a routine. The concert was being televised live and we were to be featured. Suddenly, a handsome dark-haired white man in his mid-forties rushed over to me. "Hey Arlee! Oh. Is it okay to say that?"

"Sure, I said. That's how you knew me."

"You probably don't remember me," he said awkwardly.

"Sure I do." I said. He was a former *Upbeat* clapper who used to hang around Jackie and me during rehearsals. "Now come on and dance with us John. You're the only guy dancer here today and we need you."

"Yeah!" said Jackie. "Let's dance!"

We all quickly lined up behind Hank. After taking a moment to make sure everyone was in the right position, he counted down. *"And five, six, seven, eight!"* With extraordinary vigor, he did the steps so fast I had to stop and remind him, "Hank, it's been many moons since some of us have attempted these steps. Please slow down just a little."

"Okay," he smiled understandingly then continued at the impossible pace, counting and talking as he danced. *"And five, six, seven, eight!* Popcorn! Camel walk! Moon walk! Remember, we did the moon walk *long* before Michael Jackson. In '69. I made it up right after Neil Armstrong and Buzz Aldrin walked on the moon. Only ours was different. Michael's version is like the old Marcel Marceau. *And one, two, three, four...!"*

Everyone tried hard to keep up with Hank but only Jean Hagedorn knew all the steps—apparently because she had never stopped doing them. Eventually, it all came back to the rest of us and before long we were time-warped back to the fabulous sixties. It felt fantastic! As I kicked and spun, I looked to either side. The big smiles on my fellow dancers' faces showed they were having as good a time as I was—especially Hank. As I danced I thought: about my departed friends Jim and Bev, about how good it felt to see everyone, about how wonderful it felt to be dancing again. But mostly, I thought about Arlee—about how he loved to dance. I even visualized him, doing the shiver. I left the Rock and Roll Hall Of Fame that night beaming, feeling extremely proud of my life as Arlee. The following day there were spots on the news and articles in the newspaper about *Upbeat* being honored with shots of the dancers dancing backstage. Those couple of days had been some of the best. Besides dancing with my old gang from *Upbeat* once again, it was a chance to reconnect with my past.

After living mostly in the country for five years, in September 2004 I decided to go back to New York. Three years after terrorists flew planes into the Twin Towers, killing nearly three thousand people, things were getting back to normal—although a different normal. New York was now on constant alerts and our country was at war in Iraq. It was good to be back though. I had missed Bas, who stayed mostly in New York during my stint in the country. Even though our marriage might not have been something I would have chosen under ideal circumstances, Bas always believed in me. For that I loved him. Together we purchased an eight-room co-op in Manhattan (for a ridiculously low price), which I was eager to decorate. I was also eager to get my manuscript published. It's ironic that I had once worked so hard to keep my past a secret and now am proud enough to share it with the world. Now fifty-one, I claim my past, accept the present, and prepare and pray for the future. With no idea of what life holds, I have the faith and courage to face my problems and deal with them—head on.

THE NEXT GENERATION. Bottom right; On "Black Minz" promo poster, sister Deb dancing with her daughter Hope. Far left, top; Deb's grandson Jontel, at age five the youngest member of Black Minz dance troupe.

YOU CAN ORDER *SHE CAN GO WHERE PRETTY GIRLS GO* BY MAILING CHECK OR MONEY ORDER TO:

BEYOND INK
P.O. BOX 1644
NEW YORK, NY 10026-1644

OR PHONE:

(212) 222-3704
OR
(727) 824-0820

THANK YOU!